MW00911125

DISCOVER YOUR MAGIC

CHAPTERS

Contents	Page

> *"A man travels the world over in search of what he needs, and returns home to find it."*
>
> **George Moore**

FOREWORD

In February I was on an expedition cruise liner, the ms Bremen in the Antarctic in Paradise Bay, having just visited the Argentinean Research Station. It was a sunny crisp day with penguins playing on the ice and the sun reflecting a fantastic array of colours of the various ice bergs scattered around the bay. I realised that I was looking at the edge of the earth, the sights were mind-blowing and the power and majesty of the ice unnerving. This was nature at its rawest ! Years of travelling to the world's most exotic and isolated areas have made me constantly aware of this.

"Sounds great, doesn't it ?" In fact it may sound like a dream to you. To me it is normal. Not, 'was' normal …. It still is today ! For the last fifteen years I have travelled to over 117 countries and visited some of the remotest, and most exotic places on this globe. Not because I am an adventurer or research professor for some university. Nor have I been given some great gift by a rich relative. In fact I have accomplished this by following my heart and some very basic simplistic principles.

When asked what my occupation is, and how I got to travel to all these fantastic places, I have learnt to sit back and smile at the reactions when I reveal all. "Huh ! Is that a real job ? How can you make money with that ? Don't you have a mortgage to pay every month ?" When they hear what I have accomplished, not just financially, but with all my travels and experiences, and at a very young age, their mouths are usually hanging on the floor.

Why ? Because I am a conjuror, more popularly known as a magician ! No ! Not quite your kiddie's party type magician, but a corporate illusionist who entertains and trains people in a professional environment. By using magic as a medium and a tool, combined with my academic and entertainment experience, I add a unique touch to business presentations, Master of Ceremony work, Conference Chairman or Motivational & Team Building lectures. In fact I now offer a complete 3 in 1 package of all of the above.

Initially I started out as a magician working in the British Working Men's Club circuit and television in the UK. Then I began performing as a cruise ship magician, entertaining passengers on many of the world's top cruise ships such as the Hanseatic, QE2, Vistafjord, Crystal Symphony, etc. for many years.

Can you imagine the surprise of my school colleagues, peers and family when I decided to seek fame and fortune in the global market place as a magician. They all laughed at me and told me to go get a degree and a 'professional' career !

Today, they cannot believe their eyes !

"How did you do it ? Who did you sleep with ? You are so lucky ! From whom did you inherit money ? Did you sign a pact with the Devil ?" etc. etc.

These are the comments I hear the whole time. I still have family in Germany that wants to know when I am going stop this nonsense and get a proper job !

I definitely do not see myself as being different to anyone else. However, I also don't see myself as being part of the herd. But I do believe in following one's heart. That wealth lies within and not without, or in materialistic desires. If you are true to yourself, from within, it doesn't matter who you are or what you do, true happiness will follow.

The funny thing is, that all my life, I simply followed my heart, believed in myself and never gave up !
And if I managed to achieve my dreams, with a profession like mine – YOU CAN TOO !

My main objective with this book is to give you simple, practical and effective advice, based on personal experience which will be easy for you to remember and even easier to put into practice.

What better way to do this, than to stick with the magic theme. I want to make a "magician" out of you, so that you have the power to change your own life. Therefore, I am going to use the word, "MAGICAL" as an acronym.

Every letter will stand for one point and each point will be one chapter in this book. So once you have read everything, you simply have to think back to the word, "magical" and everything will come back to you ... like magic !

During the last few years the pure passion and pleasure of sharing insights and changing peoples lives for the better, has been the most awesome gift life has given me.

Life is indeed so full of magic and if you follow your heart and give unconditionally I feel it just becomes better and better.
I have learnt that when you speak to people from your heart, and from pure personal experience to which others can relate, you begin touching souls and changing lives.

Laughter of course plays a huge role. By making my delegates laugh, their hearts open and they become so much more embracing of the insights I want to share.

This constant exposure to a global market and sharing information at conferences worldwide, has prompted me to

11

update and add so many more pages which I trust will have a great positive impact on you.

In fact my Keynote Presentations on this book have now become whole day training workshops, where I guide delegates through life changing and insightful experiences, and give them real sustainable and practical life skills which can change their lives forever.

All that is left for me to say is that I sincerely trust, you will benefit from the insights shared in this book, and that you will learn how to DISCOVER YOUR MAGIC.

Warmest wishes

Wolfgang Riebe

DISCOVER YOUR MAGIC

M = MOTIVATION

What are some of the characteristics of motivated & successful people ? What makes them tick ? What are their philosophies in life ?

Are they really that different from others ? Were they born that way ? Were they part of that lucky sperm packet ? Or are they just people like you and me that have dreams and do things slightly different from the rest of the world ?

Once you have a slight insight into this, then we can discuss the various ways and tips which will enable you to fulfil your dreams.

There are many definitions out there as to what motivates and creates a winner. My favourite is :

There are 3 kinds of motivated people in the world today :

  A. The few that makes things happen;
  B. The many who watch things happen;
  C. And the majority that had no idea that anything happened at all.

So, which group do you fall in ?

Over the years of globetrotting and literally meeting thousands of successful and wealthy people, speaking to them and feeding off their knowledge and advice, I have nurtured a few really important points which have assisted me in achieving many of my goals.

Furthermore, I believe that these tips are sound, logical and can influence your life in a positive manner, enabling YOU to become part of that select few, group 'A' people that are the leaders and make things happen.

"So ! Let us look at some of the characteristics of motivated successful people."

Characteristic No. 1 :
THINK LOGICALLY

In today's technologically advanced world, many people have been caught in the rut of complicated thinking ! By this I mean that basic and simplistic problem solving techniques and ways of analysing life situations, have been replaced by advanced modern schools of thought.

Sales are no longer just about selling at a profit, but a maze of complex business plans which will confuse any normal person. The final goal may still be the same, but the route to achieve this has become infested with corporate hierarchy structures which not even the most highly qualified academic can understand ! "Think about this for a moment !" .... How often in the last year have you heard or seen a new invention or money making idea advertised on the Home TV channels which is so simplistic that you ask yourself, "Why didn't I think of that ?"

Sit back and contemplate about this for a while. How often has someone in your work environment come up with an incredibly simplistic solution for an impossible problem ? When this has occurred, how often have you thought to yourself, "That's so easy, why didn't I think of that ?" The same applies to breakthrough developments and ideas. Often we see a new craze, or product appear on the market which is so simplistic, and the originator earns millions in commission from it, and we want to kick ourselves for not coming up with the idea !

Therefore, one of the first characteristics I found in many successful and motivated people, is that they **think logically.**

The reason they are able to do this, is because they look at life from a different more simplistic perspective. Which brings me to two exercises I want you to try, just to give you an indication of where you stand with regard to your own logical thinking ability.

Look at the following figure :

Add one line only and change this figure into a 6 !

DISCOVER YOUR MAGIC

"Did you get it straight away, or are you still battling ?"

The solution …. Put an **'S'** in front of the **IX** making it **SIX** !
"Nobody said it had to be a straight line !"

"Here's another fun exercise which I found years ago."

According to the statistics of Andersen Worldwide, around 90%
of the professionals failed this "4 Question" exam.

Even though the questions are not that difficult, I need you to
think carefully before you answer.

> ## Question 1
> Determines whether you doing simple things
> in a complicated way.

How do you put a giraffe into a refrigerator ?

> **Correct answer ...**
> Open the refrigerator, put in the giraffe and close the door.
> (Simple enough ?)

Now that you have the idea, try Question 2.

> ## Question 2
> Determines your prudence !

How do you put an elephant into a refrigerator ?

> **Correct answer ...**
> Open the refrigerator door, take out the giraffe,
> put the elephant in, and close the door.

Don't worry if you haven't scored yet, we still have two questions to go.

> ## Question 3
> Determines whether you think Comprehensively !

The Lion King is hosting an animal conference, all the animals attend except one. Which animal does not attend ?

> **Correct answer ...**
> The Elephant ! (Why ?)
> The Elephant is in the refrigerator ! (duh !)

Now for the final question, and think before you answer !

> ## Question 4
> Determines your Logical Thinking Processes !

There is a river, which is filled with crocodiles. How do you manage to cross it ?

> **Correct answer ...**
> Simply swim through it.
> All the Crocodiles are attending the Animal Meeting !

So, how did you do ?

On a lighter side, here are two stories which should put logical thinking into another perspective for you.

 Two chaps sitting over breakfast, and the one says to the other, "Man I was depressed this morning, I wanted to commit suicide !" So his friend asks aghast, "No ... what happened ?" To which the first guy replies, "I decided to take 1000 Aspirin!" "Oh no, 1000 Aspirin - what happened then ?" responds the worried friend. And his mate answered, "Well, after the first two Aspirin I started feeling better !"

A silly humorous story, but one which makes logical sense ! *In the same vein the chap walks into the library, goes up to the librarian and asks, "Where are your books on suicide ?" She replies. "Get out of here ! I know your types ... you never bring the books back again !"*

Characteristic No 2 :
PASSION

So many people I meet on a daily basis hate what they do ! I cannot understand this ? How can you go through life hating what you do ? Then you are living a lie ! Life is so short as is, so why not make the most of it ?

Why have I managed to see the world and enjoy every day to the fullest ? Why do I always tell everyone I meet that I have never worked one single day in my life ? Why am I always positive and walk around with a smile on my face ?

"The answer is so simple. I love what I do ! I follow my heart ! I have to survive on this earth, so I might as well do something I like !"

Now, even if I am not the best at what I do, if I do it with passion … I am going to try so much harder than the other person who does not have that same passion. Hence ! Success must follow !

You don't have to be a highly trained academic with super high IQ to understand this.

Aah ! But most people respond to this statement that they are in such a rut and have lost their passion that it's just not worth trying anymore.

Hello ! Wake up ! Smell the roses !

First of all contemplate as to **why** you have lost your passion. You will come up with various answers and again numerous studies with highly complicated conclusions have surfaced over the years.

In my humble opinion, there is only one simplistic and logical reason why a people lose their passion in life …. They have expectations !

The world has become a fast paced society of quick fixes and 'what's in it for me' people. No one does nothing without expecting anything in return. If I am nice to you, there is always an alternative reason … I may want to sell you something, bed you, rope you into a business deal or even abuse our friendship to suit my selfish needs !   In the end, when things don't pan out the way you wanted them to … you are disappointed.

Here's another way of looking at life :

**Why not do whatever you do,
without ever expecting anything back ?**

This is called **UNCONDITIONAL LOVE.**
I do something for you because I want to do this from the depths of my heart. I have no expectations from you whatsoever !

If I DO NOT expect anything in return, how can I ever be disappointed ? Consider just the plain statistical odds of this behaviour ? You WILL ALWAYS get somebody that WILL return this unconditional love behaviour. Even if it is only one person. Because you never expected anything in return, imagine what a great gift it will be, when you do ? And it is only by living your life through your passion, that you will do things from within your heart.

 Think back to when you were a child, how often were you keen to try something, or had a dream, and when you approached your parents about this, they laughed, put you down, or basically told you to 'grow up' and not be silly ?

Think about this, and think about your children. As a child you are free, there are no restrictions – you have an imagination and believe you can do anything. So ! "Where does this belief system disappear to ? Is it something that happens naturally – or are we taught to lose it ?"

I have two daughters, Sabrina & Alexis. Their enthusiasm and excitement fascinates me … and this hasn't changed over the years. How come then, when enthusiastic kids ask their parents for support in later years, it is not given ? "I want to bake a cake mom", the child asks. "You're too young, you'll mess up the kitchen", the mother replies. After a while the child gives up asking. This behaviour is carried over through adulthood.

I look at how excited Sabrina becomes when I ask her if she wants to go to the shop with me. She hugs and kisses me and drives me crazy with excitement in the shop. For me it is a tedious task – for her it makes her day ! How many of you get excited about the routine things in life ?

Strange how we lose this as kids ! Why ? Because parents break them down. Children get excited about becoming adults, but what do the parents say ? "Wait until you turn 18 and have to pay your own rent, earn your own money, have kids to feed, etc. Then you will see how tough life really is !" Think back … can you recall your parents saying this to you ? Even worse, have you said this to your own children ?

With what kind of future vision do children grow up when exposed to this attitude ? No wonder so many adults today are sour and not motivated.

Now ! Successful people have accepted that this was part of their growing up, and have come to terms with it. Thus it is no longer a hindrance in their lives.

They now try and relearn this enthusiasm and expectancy !

Always support your children and push them to reach their dreams. No matter how irritated you are, or whether you think your child cannot do something, let them at least try !

In one of my presentations I discuss 'Passion', and speak about various ways of finding it again. One way, is to watch and learn from you children. Here I show the delegates a photo of both my girls after they had their faces painted in a shopping mall.

Sabrina & Alexis

On one occasion, I had just returned from a road show and my wife needed a break. She sent me to the mall for some groceries and asked me to take the girls along. I was also tired from the long flight home so I rushed them through the mall. As we passed a face painter, both girls excitedly begged me to have their faces done. Having been tired and not interested, I am grateful that I gave in and let them do it. Once their faces were done, they walked around so proud and looked at themselves in every shop window. That night they wouldn't wash their faces ! They wanted to go to kindergarten like this the next day.

Consider for one moment ... would you as an adult walk into the mall and have your face painted ? I can just image your response. What ! Are you crazy ? What will everyone think ?

Ask yourself honestly why you wouldn't do this ?
People may think you're crazy ... childish ... or just plain weird. And after all, this is not typical adult behaviour. If these thoughts have crossed your mind, then re-evaluate how much conditioning, society and various other socio-cultural factors have actually negatively influenced your behaviour patterns. Realistically speaking, will this behaviour stop the world from functioning ? Will it have any bad effects on those around you ? I don't think so !

23

"Oh, but it's not the done thing", I hear you say. "Aah ! So what you're telling me is that the magic and the magic of the child within you has died! Pretty sad, huh !"

For the exact same reason that you won't paint your face and are not enthusiastic about the idea, you are not enthusiastic about life anymore.

You need to rediscover this magic by hanging out with kids again. If you have children, watch them carefully and see how excited they get. Crouch down on your knees and look at the world from their angle. Go on a roller coaster ride with them and watch their excitement. Just do something very simple with them and watch how even then they get excited. Their love is unconditional. If you don't have children, visit someone who does and watch their children.

Once you have done this, observe a successful motivated person that you know. Guess what ? You will see many similarities, especially in the department of excitement, enthusiasm and determination.

Notice how successful people are always coming up with new ideas, even if a previous idea has failed ... they NEVER give up. They do things as if for the first time. At least it appears to be so because they are always excited about everything they do.

Children's fantasies always enable them to come up with new ways of keeping themselves occupied. You may have bought them the latest toys, but that pot and lid in the pantry will keep them fascinated for hours.

Hence a question : When last have you done something new ? Created a new policy at work, found a new and simpler way of solving certain problems, tried something new in bed with your spouse ?

Two years ago at a conference I bumped into a lady who had heard me speak the year before. She simply came up to me to thank me for opening her eyes. The story she shared was so touching. After seeing the pictures of my two girls with their faces painted during my presentation, this lady and her best friend went to a mall the next day and did exactly that ! They had their faces painted !

They went to visit a friend in hospital with their brightly decorated faces. The hospital staff wouldn't let them leave and took them to all the wards where they had more fun than they could ever remember.
That evening when they eventually left the hospital, they even went to dinner like this. She recalled that it was the most fun she had had since childhood. In fact at this specific conference she was the most lively person there. See ! She had rekindled her passion and zest for life. It's not hard to do.

Characteristic No. 3 :
NEVER GIVE UP

Rick Pitino once said :
"Failure is good. It's fertilizer."

That's exactly it. By failing and trying over and over, children learn and also develop the courage and persistence to achieve their goals in later life.

I watched both my girls when they just started to walk, they must have fallen hundreds of times and screamed louder every time they fell. But they never gave up. One of the reasons is that my wife and I spurred them on and gave them support so that they would be inspired to walk. Every parent does this with their kids. This is where the basics of determination is learnt.

Many successful people have failed more than anybody else. However, they never see failure as defeat. They see it as a learned lesson which is all part of growing and developing into a better human being. If something doesn't go the way you planned, sit back and analyse why it went wrong.

Ask others around you as well. Often you don't look at your own mistakes in an objective fashion and it takes others to point out the obvious. But once you have identified what went wrong, you are in the position to try again.

I take myself trying to learn a simple sleight of hand trick where I make a coin vanish. If I give up after a few days when training my hands to become accustomed to new grips and moves - I'll never get the trick right ! But if I sit it through and practice until it's perfect, then I have a trick I can entertain my clients with for life.

 Take these modern computer adventure games. Why are they so popular with the youth ?

Have you ever tried to play one ?
Boy ! Are they difficult. Often one has to play a level over and over again until one defeats all obstacles. Only then can one proceed to the next level. Imagine if everyone gave up the game

after the first failed attempt ! But we don't ! After all how can you let a mechanical device such as a computer outwit you ? Yet we want to give up on life which is the most precious thing we have !

See your life as a game where you will play until you win ! You'll be amazed at how easy it will become to pick yourself up and learn from mistakes and try again.

Characteristic No. 4 :
STAY INFORMED

No matter what you do, most people become complacent. Again due to a lack of passion. If you love what you do you will constantly read up and stay informed about new developments, and hence always stay ahead of trends.

If you look at the baby boomer generation, change is the biggest challenge. Today's youth have accepted this as part of their life and they understand the concept of having to stay ahead of the game more than their parents. Just look at computers. Memory, operating systems and software are changing daily. If you don't keep up and inform yourself on a regular basis you will be left behind. Can anyone today really afford not to take refresher courses and at least try and keep abreast of software updates which occur every few months ?

Successful people make a point of knowing what is going on in their industry and constantly keep themselves updated and informed as to new market trends, software and products. I take myself as a celebrity TV magician. Years ago the classic top hat and tails act with silks and appearing doves was the in thing. Today's youth won't quite laugh at it, but neither will they make a special effort to watch it either. As someone who has had

27

regular prime time TV series and still works on new concepts, I have to take the youth into consideration. They are becoming the new mass market.

My first two TV series of Abracadabra was a fun family series with many classic tricks and I found that my market was children, baby boomers and their parents. In fact by researching my target market I ended up having huge viewer ship ratings and we ran for nearly 2 years with two series and 26 episodes later.

Look 'No Mirrors' – It's real !

However, the market between teenager to 28 year old, was not really into it. I had to inform myself and learn about this market. Then I produced my new high tech specials, Master Magician Wolfgang Riebe, with a high tech Matrix/Blade image. Leather pants, long jackets and tattoo (Sprayed on !) Suddenly my viewer ship ratings hit new highs, because I had included this group of viewers as well. Simple logic !

The Tattoo is fake !

Characteristic No. 5 :
MULTI-FACETED
BUSINESS APPROACH

This is the last point in this chapter and goes hand in hand with being informed. If you don't know what is going on around you, how can you adapt and change to fit in with constant changing business trends.

Again I take myself as an example. Yes ! I started out as a magician. Today I am a motivational speaker. I host conferences as Master of Ceremonies / Conference Chairman and Continuity Person. I am the star of my own TV shows, plus offer Memory Improvement as well as Whole Day Training Seminars. Someone that doesn't know me could easily accuse me of being a 'Jack of All Trades' !

Quite understandably so. But look at the bigger picture...

I started my career as a magician and realised my dreams by following this basic passion. During this time I saw the world, travelling on cruise liners and working at international conferences.

However, shortly after starting on cruise liners as a guest entertainer and only performing 2 to 3 nights per cruise, I became bored. Being a typical 'A Type' personality, I made the most of the situation.

It was every magicians dream to work on cruise ships and live with the rich and famous, see the world … and get paid to do it too ! But I never realised that there was so much free time involved. After all, there were dancers, comedians, singers,

bands and a whole host of other entertainers on board and we were all scheduled to perform at different times during the cruise.

Initially, sleeping late and tanning in the sun sounds exotic. After one month it's not so great anymore. Boredom soon set in, which left me with two choices. Party and waste my life away, or make the most of all the free time I had.

I always wanted to write articles and come up with my own new tricks and ideas and have them published in magazines world-wide for magicians. I yearned for that recognition of giving something back to the art form that had been so great to me. So I started writing ! Three years later, while travelling the world, I had tons of articles, written 20 books on the field of magic and also completed my degree in psychology and communication via correspondence. I was fulfilling my dream.

It did not stop there. I started finding out about other jobs on board such as that of the Cruise Director. Maybe I could be entertainer and cruise director ? This became my goal. It would keep me busier during the day and I could only benefit from this learned experience. After all the Cruise Director runs the entire entertainment department, hosts various activities and functions, and as an entertainer. Thus this would further enhance my communication skills.

I loved what I was doing, but wanted more. I wanted adventure and growth ! What about the smaller exclusive expedition style ships with only a handful of passengers that could sail to ports which the huge commercial liners could never visit ? Aah ! A new challenge. Imagine, being an entertainer, cruise director and expedition leader on a small ship which would do expeditions right up the Amazon, into the Antarctic, the Saigon Delta, etc. etc.

With thousands of King Penguins : South Georgia Islands near the Antarctic

How much fun it would be to take the zodiacs (rubber ducks) and do mini expeditions from the ship, listen to specialist lecturers on the fauna, flora and wild life of the regions we were visiting, enter waters no one had explored before ... and still experience all of this while magic was still the basis for landing me the job ? Wow !

Of course many adventures and even life threatening situations (more of those later) arose out of this. I eventually settled down to start a family, had a plethora of experiences which all naturally built up from my basis of magic. Companies started to book me to entertain at their conferences. Naturally I would end up chatting with everyone, and my world travels and experiences would come to light. It was only natural for one of my clients to suggest that I should offer an inspirational lecture on these adventures.

31

Corporate delegates were tired of standing on chairs, clapping hands and paying big bucks for the 3 day quick fix guys, that simply had the gift of the gab and no real life experiences. They wanted someone that could walk the walk, talk the talk, and share basic passions, which everyone could relate to. Above all, someone that could inspire through passion, conviction and self belief. A person who had lived a life of constant change, and could teach others to do the same. Someone with a magical story !

People started booking me for either, entertainment, or as a speaker. With logical thinking being one of my stronger points, I realised that I could offer a whole package to companies including the hosting of their functions as Continuity Person.

Well, the rest is history !

It was challenging entering the Keynote Speaking market as there were so many speakers on offer. Yes ! I was the star of my own TV shows. Yes ! I had performed nearly everywhere in the world, but that wasn't good enough reason for me to become an inspirational speaker. I had used my experiences and talents to grow within myself. Now I could give back to humanity by teaching love and goodwill for all future generations. Could I truly practice what I preached ? Could I speak from the heart and mean every word I say with passion ? As you read earlier, I have always only done things because of my internal belief and passion. If my goal is fuelled by a desire to give back to society, without any expectations in return – then I am on the right track.

People started talking about my presentations, and word of mouth referrals where building my reputation as a keynote speaker. I started offering the package of all my talents. I now introduced the concept of a multifaceted business approach ! I knew full well that there are times when companies will book entertainment only. But there are also times such as the beginning of the year when employees come back from holiday and need to be inspired. Here ! Motivation takes priority over entertainment.

Conferences and seminars all need an Emcee, Keynote Speaker and Entertainer. With today's flight costs and limited budgets companies are often forced to cut back. If they can save flights and accommodation, and have one man to do the job of three – it's a done deal !

Thus, by informing myself as to market trends, falling back on life's experiences and having a multifaceted business approach, I can now offer an all-in-one package to the benefit of these companies and myself.

My whole life had been about adapting to different situations, countries, audiences and cultures. I was used to change. Therefore, today I am the "Change Management Expert" and bill myself as the 3 – 1 in one "Enter-Trainer".

I identified and captured a niche market !

Everything arose from the foundation of magic, yet so diverse, and based on personal experience because of an internal passion. I have now opened a huge new market for myself, simply by applying basic logic. You can do it too !

Because of the above, I have identified my true passion. In my early twenties I would have told you that my life was all about conjuring and magic tricks. Today I have learnt that it is communication, and making the world a better place to live in.

Magic has been the medium which I use, to do this with. As I have grown and learnt about life, so has my insight and focus. I believe that if everyone of us on this earth today could just try

DISCOVER YOUR MAGIC

and change one person's attitude to the positive – we'd have heaven on earth tomorrow !

To summarise :

> **Think Logically**
> **Have Passion**
> **Never Give Up**
> **Be and Stay Informed**
> **Apply a Multifaceted Business Approach**

The above points should provide a sound foundation from which to work and give you much food for thought. Of course I have mentioned only a few of the characteristics which motivated people display, and have not yet told you how YOU can achieve this.

Don't fear, my aim with the first chapter is to create an awareness within yourself. From here on I will be giving you all the tips and tricks so that you can put this into practice.

> *"Don't be too busy making a living,*
> *that you forget to make a life."*
> **Unknown**

Notes

A = AWARENESS

 Naturally ! As a magician, I feel the above quotation is very applicable to me as a person that also does card tricks ! Each and every person on this planet can play a bad hand well, by being prepared for any eventuality. Preparedness only comes about by being aware of what is going on around you.

Let's test YOUR awareness !
Add the numbers below audibly (not in silence) and quickly.

> **1000**
> **40**
> **1000**
> **30**
> **1000**
> **20**
> **1000**
> **10**

What is your answer ?

Did you get 5000 ?

I have done this to audiences of a few thousand delegates at a time, and every time, everyone shouts a total of 5000 ... and with confidence !

The actual answer is **4100** !

Add it up again ... the second last total is 4090, plus 10 which equals 4100.

Don't you believe me ? Go back to the previous page and check again !

Now comes the big question .... Why did you say 5000 ? In a huge crowd the response is easy. You hear someone else say 5000 and you follow suit. If you read this on your own and still got 5000, don't feel bad either – it happens to most people. I'll never forget doing this for a big chartered accountant's conference (about one thousand people) and everyone shouted out 5000. You should have been there ! I never let them live it down ! Their reaction to it was just as funny – they couldn't believe they all fell for it.

Let's go back to that simple invention you saw advertised on the home shopping channel ... the one you could have invented due to it's simplicity ... but didn't ! That multi million dollar gadget which is making someone else rich today. Why did that person come up with the idea and not you ?

Simple – they were more aware ! They wouldn't have fallen for the 4100 trick either !

Here is another sentence I would like you to read.
I want you to begin reading immediately once you turn the page.
Read it out aloud and do so two or three times.

**Paris
in the
the Spring**

Did you notice something strange ? If not, read the sentence again.

If you did notice the two **"the"** words, excellent. You see, most people read a sentence like this and somewhere in their subconscious they assume that it must contain only one **"the"** and hence only read it as such. The majority of people need to read this sentence a few times before realising that **'the'** is repeated.

It is a matter of awareness. Certain people have managed to train themselves to become slightly more aware than the majority of the population, and hence are 'one step ahead'.

As I mentioned in the previous chapter, that is part of the reason why many people through 'logical thinking' appear to come up with solutions and ideas which we see as simplistic. It doesn't help if we think, "I could have done that – it's so simple", because in essence, if you are not slightly more aware than your fellow man, you are not going to do this.

So, the big question, "How do **you** become more aware ?"

When writing about motivation, many people consider it to be something one reads in order to build one's wealth, or maybe learn some tips to become wealthier.

Before one can even touch on the subject, you have to decide for yourself what the word 'wealth' actually means to you. Define wealth in your own terms, and then only read further. Allow me to take you to a new level of awareness as to what the term wealth really means.

From London I went directly onto cruise liners as a magician. I had never worked on a cruise ship before. Only a small percentage of the world's population has ever been fortunate enough to experience a cruise – yet it is one of the fastest growing industries in the world today.

Nevertheless, consider for one moment, cruises being as expensive as they are ... who can afford to go on a cruise ? Only retired older pensioners – as they have worked and saved their whole lives. So in essence, going on a cruise today is like taking a holiday on a floating old age home !

At night the ship sails from port to port, and during the day the ship docks in the harbours, where the passengers mostly disembark the ship and climb onto a tour bus for a tour of the city, etc.

Now as an entertainer on board, we were afforded the opportunity of going on these tours together with the passengers, but free of charge. However, in return we had to do a full written report and complete a questionnaire for the cruise line to make sure that everything was as advertised.
Furthermore, we also had to make sure that at every rest or photo stop, all heads were counted on the bus, nobody went missing, and naturally assist with wheelchairs, Alzheimer's passengers, etc. etc.

I will never forget one of the first land tours I did in a port in the Caribbean. I was escorting a bus load of passengers on a city tour which included highlights of the town in the morning, and a tour of the botanical gardens in the afternoon.

In the city we went into a few shops which had hundreds of electronic gadgets. I absolutely flipped out and was overwhelmed by all the high tech stuff. Had I had the money I would have bought up half the store. The passengers on the other hand were un-phased. I thought this was due to the fact that they were used to this kind of technology.

After the tour of the town we visited the botanical gardens. I couldn't believe the amount of photos these people were taking of the trees and flowers. American tourists ? Seemed more like Japanese to me by the amount of pictures they took. They were literally freaking out over stupid little flowers. Were they nuts ? Were they smoking something I had never heard of ? I couldn't understand this. In fact I found all the flowers so boring, I swore never to escort another tour again.

It took me around 3 months before I actually asked these passengers why they found this botanical garden stuff so intriguing. Well, on hearing the first answer, I was so shocked at my arrogance and naivety, that I actually listened to them ! I was so intrigued by their answers that I started speaking to everyone over the next few months.

Remember, these people have gone through life and are near the end of their lives. They have reached a different level of consciousness than most younger people. They have lived the best part of their life and I as a youngster can only learn from their experience, so I made a point of asking everyone I spoke to, how they saw wealth.

I, the young materialistic yuppie was in for a shock.

Over the next few months 3 main points came to light which changed my life and my definition of wealth completely.

1.) Spend time with, and appreciate those close to you !

Each person said that they had worked their whole life to reach the point which they were at, now, i.e. financial freedom and retirement. In the process of achieving this, all they did was work, work, work. They never had time for family, friends and co-workers. It was all about money ! Now that they have retired and think back on their lives, they regret that they never spent more time with their spouse or their children.

Many people I met on board were alone, their spouses had died. They regretted making money their god ! If only they could have their life over they would have spent more time with the people that were important to them.

What's the point of having all the money now and no-one to enjoy it with ? This is only something one can really understand and think about once you have reached this point in life !

How often have you heard someone say ... or even worse, have you said, "I cannot believe how quick my kids are growing up !" Why would anyone say this ?

Simple ! They are never home enough to enjoy their children. They are under such intense stress and pressure that they forget to spend time with their loved ones ! Just think of business life today ! 9 to 5 doesn't exist anymore. There are business meetings which run late, evening functions such as award evenings, social events and the stresses of meeting targets. If you run your own business, then it's even worse. Business owners usually work much longer and later hours, sacrificing family time. Never realising this !

 I will NEVER forget the regret and sadness on many of the retirees faces I chatted with, when they spoke about their lives. In the beginning I could never understand why all these old people were so bitter. But once I spoke to them, it all made sense.

"Do you want to be bitter the day you retire ? Do you want to regret the missed times with loved ones ?"

Remember, one day when you are older – you can NEVER ever get your youth back. The past will always be the past !

I remember that first tour quite clearly, being irritated by all these elderly people who I had to push in wheel chairs, or herd together due to Alzheimer's, etc. etc.

Here comes the 2nd point I learnt - once I got to know them.

2.) Look after your health !

Again, all they did was work their whole lives. They never looked after their bodies. Money was the priority. Check-ups at the doctor, keeping fit and eating healthy was never important. The most important thing you have is your own body. When it packs up you die, or get seriously ill. So ! Surely it is in your own interest to look after it to the best of your abilities !

Awareness levels have changed and wellness has become part of the 21st century lifestyle. Back in the 50's and 60's it was all about survival. Once I understood this, these old passengers no longer annoyed me on the tours. In fact I started respecting them for still fulfilling their dreams and having the determination and courage to try and go on these tours. My big lesson in life !

Don't misuse your body. Don't shove anything down your throat. Become aware of preservatives and fast foods that are bad for you. Keep your heart fit and go for regular check-ups. Have you looked at all the 'bad' preservatives in food today ? Are you aware what all the different E-numbers on the packaging stand for and which are harmful ? Do yourself a favour and do some research on the internet. You will be shocked at what is in our food today.

One day when you retire, do you want to be able to enjoy your old age and be fit, or do you want bad health to restrict you ? Remember, the damage you cause to your body during your life is difficult, if not impossible to reverse when you are older.

3.) Wealth is what the universe has given us for Free !

The final point I learnt was more insightful than the previous. Now that these people had retired, had time on their side, they had time to philosophise and think about their lives. It's only when you have this amount of free time, that insights occur !

For most, the realisation that the modern world has made us completely materialistic, and has brainwashed the majority of people into becoming slaves to debt, was a huge eye opener. Everyone was so busy making money, buying the new cars, keeping up with the Jones's, or the latest computers, etc. that they lost track of the basics.

Family friends and health is what real wealth is about ! Plus the beauty of what nature has given us. Initially I couldn't understand why these old people freaked out about flowers and botanical gardens. See I was young ! I only saw modern technology as interesting. But when you lived in this rut, and now sit back and think about life, you suddenly realise, "Hey the flower on the sidewalk is beautiful. In fact it's perfect. Look at the colours, look at the perfection."

When last have you really looked at a flower, smelt it and experienced it with all of your senses ? Name me one man-made thing that can compare ?

While we are running and trying to make a living, we become less aware of the important things in life. Our priorities get screwed up. Pull back and philosophise. Just look at the eastern religions who practice meditation and quiet times. Why do they do this ? To bring you back down to earth so you can get in touch with your inner self. So that you can pull yourself free from those materialistic chains.

When I finished school and national service in South Africa, I left the country due to my disgust with the politics and government of the day. I recall saying that I would never go back. After a few years of travelling the world the South African Tourism Board's logo, "The Whole World in One Country" suddenly made sense. It is God's country and has so much beauty. When the miracle of 1994 took place and the country was given new hope, I moved back again. When I look at Cape Town's Table Mountain, it is an awe inspiring sight. No man made object can ever come close to this.

Have you ever been to Africa ? There is something about the continent, almost like a magnet which attracts you. I remember sailing on a cruise liner around the southern coast after I had been away for many years – I wanted to jump over board and swim to shore. The ruggedness of the terrain, the animals, the smell of the vegetation and the incredible African sunsets. This is when I started realising how intense and how beautiful raw nature really is.

Another one of my favourite places on this earth is the Geiranger Fjord in Norway. Stand there and behold the high rock faces on either side, the snow capped mountains in the distance. Words cannot describe it. In summer one can drive, or walk up a road from the village. When one stands 500m or 1500m above the fjord and looks down at this awe inspiring site – one truly realises where real wealth and beauty lies. Have a look at the picture on the next page and let your mind wonder free.

Geiranger Fjord : Norway

Why do so many older people cruise to Alaska ?
One of the last places I would ever have thought of visiting as a young person. Stand on a ship in Glacier bay and behold these huge million year old glaciers with the light reflecting different shades of green, blue, brown and purple off the ice. Listen to the sound of thunder as the ice carves and falls into the ocean. It's like someone sticking an electric cable into you and charging you up. Now that's true wealth and power !

Glacier Bay : Alaska

We buy our children all the latest toys and computer games to keep them out of our hair. Ask them what they really want ! To play with you as the parent and spend time in the park or at the beach doing this. That balance has disappeared. Go back to basics and savour the things in life that cost nothing.

Flowers, trees, oceans, mountains, that which nature had made, is more beautiful and refreshing than anything else. One of the most beautiful botanical gardens I ever visited was Butchard Gardens in Victoria, Canada. Again, words cannot describe the beauty of the flowers and the scenery.

Butchard Gardens : Victoria : Canada

DISCOVER YOUR MAGIC

To be one with the universe and nature took the elderly their whole lives to learn. Don't make the same mistakes.

> **Act now**
> **Appreciate the people close to you**
> **Look after your body**
> **Enjoy what the universe has put on this earth for you.**

To summarise :
I received a wonderful poem via email from the Journal of Humanistic Psychology. Written by an 85 year old man who puts life into perspective.

IF I HAD MY LIFE TO LIVE OVER

If I had my life to live over again, I would try to make more mistakes next time. I'd try not to be so damned perfect; I'd relax more, I'd limber up.

I'd be sillier than I've been on this trip; In fact, I know of very few things I'd take quite so seriously; I'd be crazier ... and I'd certainly be less-hygienic; I'd take more chances ... I'd take more trips ...

I'd climb more mountains ... I'd swim more rivers ... And I'd watch more sunsets; I'd burn more gasoline, I'd eat more ice cream - and fewer beans; I'd have more actual troubles and fewer imaginary ones,

You see, I was one of those people who lived sensibly, hour-after-hour and day-after-day; Oh, that doesn't mean I didn't have my moments, but if I had it to do all over, I'd have more of those moments, In fact, I'd try to have nothing but wonderful moments, side-by-side.

47

> *I was one of those people who never went anywhere without a thermometer, a hot water bottle, a gargle, a raincoat and a parachute; If I had it to do all over again, I'd travel lighter next time.*
>
> *If I had my life to live all over again, I'd start barefoot earlier in the spring and I'd stay that way later in the fall; I'd play hooky a lot more.*
>
> *I'd ride more merry-go-rounds, I'd pick more flowers, I'd hug more children, I'd tell more people that I loved them, If I had my life to live over again. But, you see, I don't.*

Once you grasp and truly understand the concept of the above story, contentment and happiness follow naturally.

Think about it, can money really buy you health and happiness ? I don't think so ! And best of all, once this philosophy becomes part of your life, the universe starts looking after you !

A friend recently visited me who had worked on cruise ships. He was a bit sad that he only had photos of people he met, and not the scenery.

I still laughed and said to him, *"The places you have been to, you can download all those photos off the internet at any time and relive those moments. You can actually sense the picture with all 5 senses, because you have been there. But your friends and the people you met, the good times you had, those photos you cannot download again – those are the photos you will want to look at again in years to come and remember the wonderful friendships you created. You did right to take those and keep those – they are precious – friends are precious !"*

O. A. Battista has a quote which can also be added to the above example :

> *"The greatest weakness of most humans is their hesitancy to tell others how much they love them while they're still alive."*

Thomas Carlyle puts it all in one nutshell :

> *"The tragedy of life is not so much what men suffer, but rather what they miss."*

To be truly successful, get your priorities in order, and the money will follow naturally !
Here's an incredible story a friend sent me via email many years ago, and to this day I find that it really puts life on this earth into perspective.

WHAT ARE THE REAL 7 WONDERS OF THE WORLD ?

A group of university students were asked to list the present Seven Wonders of the World. The following got the most votes:

1. Egypt's Great Pyramids
2. Taj Mahal
3. Grand Canyon
4. Panama Canal
5. Empire State Building
6. St. Peter's Basilica
7. China's Great Wall

While gathering the votes, the teacher noted that one quiet student hadn't turned in her paper yet. So she asked the girl if she was having trouble with her list. The girl replied, "Yes, a little. I couldn't quite make up my mind because there were so many." The teacher said, "Well, tell us what you have, and maybe we can help."

The girl hesitated, then read, "I think the Seven Wonders of the World are :

1. to touch
2. to taste
3. to see
4. to hear

She hesitated a little, and then added

5. to feel
6. to laugh!
7. and to love

The room was so full of silence you could have heard a pin drop. Those things we overlook as simple and "ordinary" are truly wondrous.

A gentle reminder that the most precious things are right in front of your eyes :

Your family
Your faith
Your love
Your health
Your friends

I feel that adding these stories to my book, just brings so much more punch to the message, I am trying to share with you. So often, friends from all over the world send me these, and my jaw drops as I am awed by their lessons.

More people all over the world should do this in order to constantly remind their friends of these lessons. It's all good and well to be sending jokes and funnies by mail, but the occasional touching stories emailed to the right friends at right time can start a whole snowball effect and really change the world.

On that note, here's another one I have to share with you ... it deals with the rules of happiness.

THE RULES OF HAPPINESS

1. *Free your heart from hatred.*
2. *Free your mind from worries.*
3. *Live simply.*
4. *Give more.*
5. *Expect less.*

What the heart gives away is never gone... It is kept in the hearts of others.

Remember that great love and great achievements involve great risks.

Secure a special place in your heart...a certain place only you can enter.

For there will come a time when you need to find yourself and only your heart will show you the way.

The measure of love is when you love without measure. In life, there are very few chances that you'll meet the person you love and who loves you in return. So once you have it, don't ever let go...The chance might never come your way again.

People are made to be loved and things are made to be used. That's why there's so much chaos in the world... people are being used and things are being loved.

You cannot finish a book without closing its chapters. If you want to go on, then you have to leave the past as you turn the pages of life. Every commitment is a choice. Non-choosers and half-choosers are a puzzle to themselves and to others.

They live in the immature condition of wanting to "play everything by ear."

Every once in a while ask yourself the question :

1. *If money weren't a consideration, what would I like to be doing ?*

2. *It's better to lose your pride to the one you love, than to lose the one you love because of pride.*

3. *We spend so much time looking for the right person to love... or finding fault with those we already love... when instead, we should be perfecting the love we give.*

4. *When you truly care for someone, you don't look for faults...You don't look for answers... you don't look for mistakes. Instead, you fight the mistakes, you accept the faults, and you overlook excuses.*

This now brings me to my second main topic under awareness … something which I know YOU can relate to !

HATRED !

"Do you know somebody that you don't like ?" Be honest ! This could be a family member, co – worker, boss, politician, actor, etc. When you see this person your blood boils. You immediately tense up. We all know someone like this.

I call them people we love to hate !

Now I want you to consider the following statement :

"If you hate someone, or something, that person or thing has a power over you"
Unknown

This has always been one of my favourite sayings, and even though it was known to me, it took a long time for me to learn the true meaning of it.

I want you to carefully consider another question ….

What is the one asset in life that is irreplaceable ?

Think very carefully before answering, as there is only one correct answer !

The most valuable asset you have in life is ...

TIME !

Why ? Because you don't know how much of it you are going to have ! Nobody knows how long they will live, or when they will die. You could be dead tomorrow morning from a heart attack … you don't know this !

TO REALIZE

To realize the value of ONE YEAR, ask a student who failed a grade.

To realize the value of ONE MONTH, ask a mother who gave birth to a premature baby.

To realize the value of ONE WEEK, ask the editor of a weekly newspaper.

To realize the value of ONE HOUR, ask the lovers who are waiting to meet.

To realize the value of ONE MINUTE, ask a person who missed the train.

To realize the value of ONE SECOND, ask a person who just avoided an accident.

To realize the value of ONE MILLI-SECOND, ask the person who won a silver medal in the Olympics.

Yes, this puts time into a simple perspective, but to realise the 'real' value of time, read this next story by another unknown author. It's one of those stories that will not only bring tears to your eyes, but you will remember it for the rest of your life. In fact, every married couple needs to read this !

TAKE HOLD OF EVERY MOMENT

A friend of mine opened his wife's underwear drawer and picked up a silk paper wrapped package :

"This, - he said - isn't any ordinary package." He unwrapped the box and stared at both the silk paper and the box.

"She got this the first time we went to New York, 8 or 9 years ago. She has never put it on. She was saving it for a special occasion. Well, I guess this is it." He got near the bed and placed the gift box next to the other clothing he was taking to the funeral house, his wife had just died. He turned to me and said :

"Never save something for a special occasion. Every day in your life is a special occasion." Those words changed my life.

Now I read more and clean less.

I sit on the porch without worrying about anything.

I spend more time with my family, and less at work.

I understand that life should be a source of experiences to be lived up, not survived through.

I use crystal glasses every day.

I'll wear new clothes to the supermarket, if I feel like it.

55

I don't save my special perfume for special occasions, I use it whenever I want to.

The words "Someday..." and "One Day..." are fading away from my dictionary. If it's worth seeing, listening or doing, I want to see, listen or do it now.

I don't know what my friend's wife would have done if she knew she wouldn't be there the next morning. This nobody can tell. I think she might have called her relatives and closest friends.

She might call old friends to make peace over past quarrels !

I'd like to think she would go out for Chinese, her favorite food.

It's these small things that I would regret not doing, if I knew my time had come.

I would regret it, because I would no longer see the friends I would meet, letters that I wanted to write, "One of these days".

I would regret and feel sad, because I didn't say, enough times, to my brothers and sisters, family and friends, how much I love them.

Now, I try not to delay, postpone or keep anything that could bring laughter and joy into our lives. And, each morning, I say to myself that this is a special day !

A classic saying, which I am sure you have heard, puts this nicely into perspective :

> *Yesterday is history, tomorrow is the future and today is a gift ... that is why it is called the present !*

How often has someone in your work environment annoyed you, or even a family member ? Every time you have anything to do with that person you feel aggression or hatred towards him/her. In other words, you spend time telling others what a schmuck this person is, or you just build up bad thoughts in your own mind.

What are you doing ? You are giving of the most precious thing you have ... your life's time .... To bitch and moan about someone else !

Isn't that completely stupid ?

Imagine you spent the last 5 minutes of your life complaining about someone you didn't like and then died ! Imagine you could get a second chance and get that time back ... would you then rather have held a loved one in your arms and told them you loved them ?

The answer is obvious !

By giving any time to people or things you hate, you are giving them a power over you.

Look at the world today filled with it's hatred and wars. It has really become a sad state of affairs. Now imagine if everyone suddenly stopped living in the past, lived for today and enjoyed the moment. It would become paradise on earth !

There will be people now and in the future that will hurt you, but your response and attitude toward them is what will make you sink or float at the end of the day. It is your awareness of the situation and life as a whole, that will be the difference in whether you impulsively react negatively, or simply let go of this hatred and transform that negative energy into positive energy.

Eleanor Roosevelt also found a great way to put it :

> *"No one can make you feel inferior without your consent."*

This can be best explained by means of a personal example.

I am German, but was brought up in South Africa and as mentioned previously, left the country due to the apartheid government of the day. I headed for England to seek fame and fortune as a magician. The initial road to success for myself had many obstacles and pitfalls including many nights of sleeping on stations in London and having no money for food. There were times I would walk down a high street and offer restaurants a show in return for food only.

Even the doves on Trafalgar Square had more food than me !

58

As I had been brought up in South Africa and learnt English there, I understandably had a South African English accent. Hence every time I opened my mouth in England, the British recognised the accent and labelled me a racist. To cover myself, I would immediately respond that I was German and had only been brought up in South Africa ..... the British now hated me **even more** !

I laugh about it now, but it was quite a thing for me then. How could I get ahead if a silly thing such as my accent and background stood in the way. After all I had just left one country because of racism, and now it was being thrown in my face in another country. The easy way out would have been to hate the British as well and simply move to Germany.

Pretty much a catch 22 situation. I have always believed that whatever situation you find yourself in, try pull away and look at it from an outsider's point of view. Become objective. This enabled me to analyse my situation. I loved the British sense of humour – at least they had a sense of humour ! The German's don't have one .... and when they do, it's very precise ! So what could I do to make the most of my circumstances ?

Remember that you also have to take responsibility in your own life. Today it has become so easy to blame one's parents, the previous governments, etc. Hence the appearance, of all these human rights groups which in my opinion are mostly founded on hatred from the past. If I wanted happiness, I would have to find it. No one else would do it for me. I had to pull my finger from my rear end and I had to make the effort !

What options did I have ? Firstly I had to learn to speak like they did. Make myself easier understood. Learn about their culture and try fit in. Boy it's amazing how quickly things start turning around when you take the first step. Suddenly people warmed to me.

DISCOVER YOUR MAGIC

Yes ! It did take time, but by merely becoming aware and changing my attitude, things started going better.

At that time everyone was boycotting anything to do with South Africa. The entertainment industry would black list anyone that dared perform in the South Africa. Here I was in the England which were the biggest instigators of this boycott. But I didn't give up (remember chapter one and successful people that never give up ?). I tried everything to fit in, which resulted in my being one of, if not the first, non equity member to appear on BBC television ... and that with my South African accent !

BBC's The Generation Game
with Bruce Forsyth

ITV : Channel 4's Motormouth

Eventually I managed to get well known on TV and big entertainment agents started contacting me and offering me work around the globe. One of the first big contracts I accepted was to work for Princess cruises. For years I travelled the world on luxury cruise liners from the Love Boat, QE2, Vistafjord, Crystal Symphony, Hanseatic and many more.

My wife was my assistant in my shows. I used to cut her into 4 and levitate her in the air. It still sounds funny to me when I mention that to people. I mean, how often to you hear someone say, "Hey ! I get to cut my wife in 4 for entertainment !"

We saved every cent we made, and kept our eyes open for every business opportunity we could find around the world. While our colleagues where eating ashore, spending money on luxuries and drinking their salaries away on board, my wife and I saved religiously, studied and utilised the time together to get to know each other from a deeper level.

They say that travelling the world is the university of life. When I look back today – how true it is. The more we travelled the more we both realised how much we loved Cape Town and that it was indeed one of the most beautiful cities in the world. The government of the day had changed and there was a new hope for South Africa, so we decided to ultimately move back and begin building our dream home.

And best of all, we had been working in international waters on cruise liners for many years and saved all our money. It was tax free ! And legally earned ! Don't forget that the USD / ZAR exchange was in our favour, as the South African currency was already pretty weak. So we were getting great value for our money.

We started designing our dream home. Now you must remember that having lived in hotel rooms and cruise ship cabins for so many years, we were used to small accommodation. Now we had the money, we could build our dream home. We could be excessive ! It didn't take long before we designed a mansion with all the necessities in life, such as a cinema, wine cellar, bar, gym, etc.

I'll never forget arriving back in Cape Town and seeing the project management company about building our home. They kept telling us that our dream home was too big. 1000 Square meters ! I need to clarify something here ... that's not the plot of land, that's the house itself !

Eventually they did a costing and it worked out that we didn't have enough money for our house ! We couldn't believe it ! What a shock for us !

After some serious planning and discussions, we worked out that we could travel for another year and earn the balance of the money so that we could pay everything cash, and have the house built without a mortgage. Contracts were drawn up and we put down the money we had thus far, with the project management company. They could start building. The timing would be perfect. When we came back after a year the house would be completed and we would hand over the balance of the money in return for the front door key.

We arrived back after that year, to the picture on the next page.

Our Dream Home

At this point I need to clarify something – NOT the white house at the back ! This company had disappeared with ALL OUR MONEY. A life's savings GONE. All that stood on the plot of land was some basic foundation work, as you can see in the picture above. That's my wife standing on the wall.

Now let's talk about HATRED ! You want to know what hatred is really all about ? Ask me ! I've been there ! I know ! I hated these people so much, I paid someone to hunt them down and beat the living daylights out of them...

This guy also ran away with my money !!!

For six months of my life I ran after this company. Six months of my life I lived and breathed hatred ! I can take those 6 months and throw them out of the window.

I had completely wasted this part of my life.

Eventually a friend of mine came to me and noticed my severe aggression. He still looked at me calmly and suggested I should let go of the attachment of my hatred. I wanted to smack him as well ! He was one of these 'new age' types with all sorts of alternative advice.

As I have gotten older, I have learnt to respect everyone's belief systems. And in fact his advice that day has been one of the most powerful statements I have ever heard. Once I made the effort to understand what he meant !

Let go of the attachment of the hatred !

"Let's backtrack ... why when we hate do you feel this intense internal aggression ? Why is it that your blood boils and you see no reason ?"

Hate grows in your subconscious mind. The more you feed it, the bigger it becomes. Imagine a thorn gripping itself to the inner walls of your subconscious. The more you feed it the deeper it claws into you.

Now try an exercise. When you get up in the morning, stand next to your bed and close you eyes. Visualise all that hatred within you manifesting itself in a big black ball in front of you. The blackness represents all the negativity, hate and evil feelings within you. Now imagine yourself throwing this ball away from you. As you throw it away it starts disintegrating and disappearing until it has vanished completely.

Do this every day for three weeks. It is said that it takes three weeks for any habit to form, or disappear. Therefore, by you constantly imagining yourself throwing the hatred away for a three week period, you will eventually let the grip of the hate (thorn) inside you release and disappear altogether.

I tried this, and after three weeks I suddenly felt calmer. Why – because the internal hatred (thorn) had let go. I now found myself in a position where I could suddenly think clearly. This allowed me to objectively analyse what had happen and come up with a game plan to make the best of my situation.

You see, had I not visualised myself throwing the hatred away, it would still have been stuck in me today.

 So now I could take stock and decide what to do without all the internal hatred getting in the way. I started going for brick laying courses, plumbing courses, etc. and started building the house together with my wife. We would build for 3 months and run out of money. Then we would do a three month contract at sea again, and so it went on.

There were times when I flew out on my own for 6 months at a time while my wife remained at home and attempted to supervise male chauvinistic contractors to complete certain tasks on the property. It was hard work and took lots of sacrifice.

Four years later our house was built !

Today we live in our dream home !

Here are two pictures of the Atrium and entrance to our home.

Atrium Entertainment Area   Outside side View

What's this all got to do with hate ? Quite simple .... Had I remained in that internal aggressive hateful state of mind, I would never have let go of it, nor would I have built my house.

Three things happened in my life because I became aware of my aggression and hatred. What did I do about it ?

1.) By changing my attitude and releasing the hatred I managed to learn so much about the building industry that I could not only build my own house, but also had enough knowledge to start my own building company and earn even more money than I had lost. Today, as a direct result of this I have my own property investment company and own numerous properties. None of this would ever have happened had I not converted all that negative energy into positive energy.

2.) Furthermore, by building the house on our own, we could do it in our own time. Plus we could do it as we could afford it. Therefore, we saved a lot on contractor costs and fees, as well as the possibility of getting ripped of again. By doing it this way, we made up a lot of the money we lost ... which is also positive !

3.) And finally, those of you that are married, how many of you have gone through stressful periods in your relationships ? This was DEFINITELY one of them. And we survived it ! In fact it brought my wife and I even closer together ! And that's worth all the money on earth to me !

Now when I look back, it was the best thing I ever did. Today I sit and enjoy my home, which I built, brick for brick, together with my wife. Not only do we both have a sense of accomplishment and satisfaction, but have gained so much knowledge in the process as well. Simply because we let go of our hatred, and took the power back.

> **If you hate somebody or something,
> that person or thing has a power over you !**

Let go of that hatred and see what a change you can make in your life.

Just think of what a different world we could be living in today if everyone let go of all the things that happened in the past. Recently I read a interesting article which put this into perspective for me.

People that suffer from stress are only doing so because they are worrying about the future and what is to come.

People that suffer from hatred and negative attitudes, do so solely, because they live in the past !

> **The big issue here is that you need to live in the NOW !**

And you can only do this by living in the moment. Is being negative about the past going to change anything ? What about worrying about the future ? Is that going to change what's going to happen ?

These are two huge emotions which need to be controlled. The only way you can do it is to learn from the past and get over it.

Your emphasis must be on savouring every moment of the day, and enjoying every minute. And you can only do this if you are free of hatred.

When mentioning the above example, a really good humorous quote always comes to mind, and tends to be my philosophy in life today :

> *"A positive attitude may not solve all your problems,*
> *but it will annoy enough people*
> *to make it worth the effort !"*
> **Herm Albright**

CONDITIONING !

"What is conditioning ?"
Many research studies have been done with astronomical facts and figures.

Today, humanity is a product of society and the media ! We are controlled without even realising it !

On the following page, is a classic example which defines conditioning from a corporate perspective.

COMPANY POLICY

Start with a cage containing five apes.

In the cage, hang a banana on a string and put stairs under it. Before long, an ape will go to the stairs and start to climb towards the banana. As soon as he touches the stairs, spray all of the apes with cold water. After a while, another ape makes an attempt with the same result - all the apes are sprayed with cold water. This continues through several more attempts.

Pretty soon, when another ape tries to climb the stairs, the other apes all try to prevent it. Now, turn off the cold water. Remove one ape from the cage and replace it with a new one. The new ape sees the banana and wants to climb the stairs. To his horror, all of the other apes attack him. After another attempt and attack, he knows that if he tries to climb the stairs, he will be assaulted.

Next, remove another of the original five apes and replace it with a new one. The newcomer goes to the stairs and is attacked. The previous newcomer takes part in the punishment with enthusiasm. Again, replace a third original ape with a new one. The new one makes it to the stairs and is attacked as well.

Two of the four apes that beat him have no idea why they were not permitted to climb the stairs, or why they are participating in the beating of the newest ape. After replacing the fourth and fifth original apes, all the apes, which have been sprayed with cold water, have been replaced.

No ape ever again approaches the stairs. Why not ?

Because that's the way they've always done it and that's the way it's always been around here.

And that's how company policy begins....

How often have you wanted to do something, or have come up with what you consider to be a brilliant idea ? The first thing you do is to approach family and close friends about this idea. If they indicate a negative response, and put down your ideas on a constant basis, you will eventually become fed up and just stop bothering. Why ? Because of continuous negative conditioning.

The same applies to the mass media, i.e. radio, TV and newspapers. Everyday we are exposed to the views of the mass media and in essence they very much control the way most people think. Consider the following; the media provides us with a constant flow of information regarding the high crime rate and the bad state of economic affairs, hence most people spend their time talking about these negative issues and many people are influenced to such an extent that they emigrate !

Take any newspaper and look at the first 3 pages. Most of the headings are usually about some or other idiot politician and his hare brained schemes. Or, politicians bickering at each other and shouting accusations rather than working for the people. Hiding corruption accusations, or looking after their own interests. Personally ! I could never remain optimistic if I had to read this every day.

Now ! Motivated people understand that the media controls our thoughts, attitudes and feelings in more ways than we would comfortably acknowledge. Once you have accepted this, it is easier to stand on the outside looking in. I know the media sells on sensationalism, so I avoid that section of the newspaper.

News is important to a business man. What are the world markets doing ? Where is gold at today ? Have raw material prices gone up or down ? This is objective and necessary information. But to get worked up over some self important, unproductive, political sycophant who's been pushed into a corner, that's stupid. In defence he may blame someone else from the past, to hide his incompetence and cause a great media scandal. Now most people begin believing that the country is going to the dogs. That's really dumb !

My pet example : Every day the media attempts to make people buy newspapers & watch the news through sensationalistic headings. Most of the time these are short, unrealistic and often, subjective.
In most countries we are bombarded with negative media continuously – hence creating a negative effect within society. Every day we read about the high crime rates, the bad economy and the falling currency. Hello ! What chance do you have but to become negative ! Naturally with continuous exposure, we become conditioned to believe this.

I have a theory !
If for just one week, TV, newspapers and the radio could highlight the positive side of each story they expose the masses to – what do you think would happen ?

The likelihood is very good that a new POSITIVE ATTITUDE would become apparent !

Of course the media is not the only one to blame !

It is all good and well for me to say that the media & our social circle can condition our belief system, but contentment will do this as well. Have you lived in one country all your life, or have you travelled ? If you have travelled, have you done so as a tourist, or have you actually worked in other countries ? After having travelled the world for more that twelve years and 117 countries later, we decided to move back to South Africa. Why ?

Either I was totally mad, or maybe I saw what was going on in the rest of the world and realised that the grass is not greener on the other side… if it is, you have to mow it more often !!!

Today, 12 years later I am based in Frankfurt, Germany - although I still work world wide. Why ? I was just flying too much. Living on planes and flying great distances. Now I am central, near the airport and can be anywhere in the world within 8 hours. It's just more practical, plus I have the entire European market on my doorstep and now have more time with my family – and hence more time to enjoy life to the fullest.

On that note, many people have asked me – where's the most beautiful place you have ever been ? To be honest, every country is beautiful and every country has it's unique features. But the bottom line is – it doesn't matter where you live, if you have your loved ones with you, are healthy, have stability and can make ends meet – then you can be happy.

Have you ever heard people say, "You always want what you cannot have ?" e.g. someone else's wife, or husband !!! When they do get this person, they realise that this fantasy or impression they had, is not what they expected. Often they are disappointed.

It is the same with a country, many people are caught up in their little environments, never lifting their heads and looking above the crowd, or outside their social circle – hence they live in a tunnel vision environment and only see life through their little world. Naturally they will start finding fault !

With satellite TV channels such as Discovery and National Geographic – the whole world has opened up to each and every person. Forget the soap operas for a change and watch something educational. Learn about this great world and above all – learn about how very similar we actually all are - no matter where you're from !

And the older you get the more you realise that your health, the people you love, and being able to make ends meet is about as

DISCOVER YOUR MAGIC

important as it gets. Who cares where you live. If you are happy within yourself, you can be happy in the middle of the desert !

Hence the SUCCESSFUL person, ignores nonsense like this and does not let him/herself become affected by other people's and society's belief systems. They believe in themselves and know what they are capable of.

WHAT TIME DO YOU WAKE UP ?

In my seminars I quiz my delegates as to the times they wake up in the morning. Most people wake up around 05h30, 06h00 or 06h30.

I wake up at 06h17 !

Why ?

Most people wake up to a radio alarm clock next to the bed. When they wake up on the hour or half an hour, what is the first thing they hear ? The news ! And what is the news ? Negative& Bad ! etc. etc.

When I wake up at 06h17 I usually hear music ! Whether I like the music or not is irrelevant, because whatever music is playing, it is more positive than the news.

Think for a moment … from the minute you wake up you have heard the first bad news. During breakfast you hear more. In the car on the way to work even more. By the time you have arrived in your office, how many negative news broadcasts have you heard ?

Can anyone blame you for walking into the office in an aggressive mood ?

Set your alarm just a few minutes before or after the hour or half hour, the odds of waking up to music are so much better. Have a CD in your car and switch to this when the news comes on. Remember that it's not one little thing that makes you negative in life, but a combination of many small irritations. Recondition yourself to think DIFFERENTLY to the rest of the masses. Negate all the small annoyances. Odds are ! You will become hugely more positive about life.

An old Indian chief sat in his hut on the reservation, smoking a ceremonial pipe, and eyeing two government officials sent to interview him.

"Chief Two Eagles," asked one official, "You have observed the white man for 90 years. You've seen his wars and his material wealth. You've seen his progress, and the damage he's done.""

The chief nodded in agreement. The official continued, "Considering all these events, in your opinion, where did the white man go wrong ?"

The chief stared at the government officials for over a minute and then calmly replied, "When white man found the land, Indians were running it. No taxes, no debt, plenty buffalo, plenty food, everyone helped each other to complete work, medicine man free, women at home at teepee with children, Indian man spent all day hunting and fishing, and all night having sex."

Then the chief leaned back and smiled, "White man dumb enough to think he could improve system like that."

An added point I would enjoy including is a brief look at energy. It has been proven that energy is all around us, and we are energy too. Go to your bedroom or bathroom mirror and brush your hair vigourously with a plastic comb. Do this in the dark and look at the mirror closely. You WILL see sparks flying !

Alternatively, rub a plastic ruler on your clothes and hold it above your hair – the hair stands up. We all tried this at school. Now the killer example I want you to try is to go to a 'live' (not plastic) plant in your home. Ever so slowly move your hand towards one of the leaves, then move your hand back and forward, without touching the leaf. Guess what ? … the leaf will start moving !

Why do all these things happen ? Because everything on this earth is made up of energy !

Have you ever met someone and felt drained and tired after they have left ? As if they have drained you from every last bit of energy ? Stay clear from those people ! If you are forced to have dealings with them, cross your arms in front of you when speaking to them. This blocks off the path of energy leaving your body from your solar plexus, and you should feel much better.

If you travel frequently and stay in hotels, I am sure you have had mornings where you woke up feeling drained and not recovered from the night's rest. One explanation could be that the bed in the hotel is positioned wrong. Let me explain ….. the earth is a magnet with a north pole and a south pole. We too, are magnets, our head is north and our feet are south. If your bed in your bedroom faces East to West, it is out of alignment with the earth's magnetism. Hence! When you sleep, you are out of alignment too. In a hotel it is difficult to do, but check at home, and if your bed's headboard doesn't face north, try and move it ! You will notice a difference in how you feel the next morning !

Okay, you don't have to redesign and redecorate your whole room. Some people say that placing a small pyramid under your bed (that's if it's not aligned north to south) negates the imbalance and helps as well without you having to redo the whole room.

You'll be surprised at how many business people actually travel with a small pyramid in their luggage so that they can sleep peacefully in their hotel rooms … but that's another whole book on it's own.

I know these examples may sound a little strange for some of you, but just try them, and you will be surprised at the results. After all, awareness does include a very broad spectrum of things you need to take into account, and if energy can affect you for the positive or negative, it is something you need to be aware of.

Now that I have touched on a few pointers to increase your general level of awareness as far as your internal consciousness is concerned, let me touch on practical tips which you could start to implement immediately and which will put you a few steps ahead of others around you.

I will never forget as a child, my dad taught me this next lesson, and I have practised it throughout my life. People are always surprised at how aware I am of everything around me. This always perplexes me, as this has become second nature.

Start these exercises slowly, they are easy to do. Try and think of how you see the world right now, and once you have mastered them, look back at the difference they have made.

DISCOVER YOUR MAGIC

Firstly, I would like you to find a pen and paper, then get up and walk straight out of the room, you are in at present. When outside, write down 5 things in the room which you can remember. The exact position they are in, the colour, size, etc. Go now and do it and carry on reading once you have tried this.

For those of you who attempted this exercise ... a question : Isn't it strange how difficult it is to remember even two simple items ? Especially if it is a room, or office which is strange to you. Even more scary, if you are sitting in a familiar environment – did you notice how you struggled as well ?

From now on I want you to try and remember at least 5 things when entering any new environment. For the next 3 weeks, every time you walk into a new office, shop, someone's home, etc. if possible, walk straight out and see what you can remember. Alternatively just stay standing and look in another direction, or close your eyes, and try the same.

But don't start with 5 things. Begin only with one ! You will find that it will be quite difficult and requires lots of concentration. In fact the first few days will take you very much out of your comfort zone.

Once you can comfortably enter any new environment and immediately notice one thing you never noticed before, start trying to see two things. Build this up until you can pick up 5 things instantly. It should take you around three weeks. Here we come back to the three week habit forming story again. Strange how this keeps coming back ! After three weeks you should find yourself doing this without thinking and it should be imbedded within your subconscious mind to naturally become more observant wherever you go.

Discover Your Magic

How is this going to help you ? The next time you walk into a strange office to meet a new client, or undergo an interview, etc., you will take in 5 items in the office almost instantly by the time you reach the person to shake their hand. Hence as an example you would have noticed the picture on the desk of this person's wife and 3 children. Also you would have picked up the Personnel Management diploma on the wall and the recent Team-building certificate next to it. He may even have a World Cup Football jersey hanging on his wall signed by the whole winning team. Also, he may have a laptop, or computer standing on his desk.

The average person enters a stranger's office, focusing their attention on the person behind the desk and see nothing else, if very little around them. In your new more aware and heightened state of mind, by the time you have reached the desk and shaken the hand of this person, you have gained 5 facts, that most people have not trained themselves to do.

Immediately, you have the upper hand. You already know that this person is married with 3 children and has a diploma in personnel management. He has also taken part in a Team Build (and is proud of it, otherwise the certificate wouldn't be hanging on the wall), is a AVID rugby fan (as this jersey is like gold to the die hard fans and hard to obtain) and must be computer literate because of the laptop on the table. This could further mean he may be using email, and for contact purposes, it would not be inappropriate to ask for his email number.

Alternatively, imagine an estate agent walking into a house for the first time. By training him/herself to be aware and pick up at least 5 things inside the house before speaking to the client, they also manage to be one ahead. For example, they walk in and notice the smell of fresh paint (something could have been recently covered up), along the cornice in the entrance hall they see some moss (a sign of damp), a dog is at the door (pets living in the house), the furnishings are very sparse (client may need to sell and short of cash), the plaster doesn't match up along one of the walls (could be a recent repair).

These are simple points one could pick up within seconds once the door has been opened, and have already made the estate agent aware of certain facts in the house. Thus, when the house owner immediately starts telling the agent that they never had damp problems and nothing has been touched up in the house, the agent knows the current owner could be lying and hence must be careful what to believe or not.

By training yourself to do this – you are not one, BUT five steps ahead of others. What is one of the secrets to success ? Being one step ahead of others !

These two examples are very simple, but should bring across the importance of this exercise. Once you have trained yourself to remember these things, you will notice that your subconscious will automatically take over and you will start picking up and noticing things you never thought relevant before. When walking into an office pool, you will subconsciously remember the first 5 things you see. Later on when thinking back to that office pool you will recall, "Hey ! They didn't have a fire extinguisher on any of the walls, nor were there emergency exit signs in case of a fire." Now you could go back and sell them a fire extinguisher. You saw a gap in the market by simply being aware !

What about peoples names ? The nicest thing you can hear on this earth is the sound of your own name ! In today's society where business is about numbers and turnover, personal relationships with clients tend to take a back seat. Fortunately in my business and the fact that I communicate directly with people every day, I have learnt the importance of giving that personal service and showing a personal interest in everyone I meet. For me, first impressions are important. And if I want to talk about caring about the world, I need to practice what I preach. Remembering someone's name is really important for me.

Be honest, how often has a stranger been introduced to you, and not even 2 seconds later, you have forgotten their name ? Ha, forget the 2 seconds, … as this person says the name, you already forgot !

As we become a smaller global village and get exposed to people from different cultures and races, especially those we are unfamiliar with, names become even more difficult to remember. Suddenly we start using general terms for everyone we meet. "Hi mate !" This is far easier to say than remembering the name, especially if it's a foreign name. "Hey girl, let's talk about yesterday's meeting." Sound familiar ?

I believe that the MINIMUM RESPECT you can show any other person on this planet, is to at least MAKE AN EFFORT to try and remember their name. It doesn't matter who you are or where you come from. If I respect you as a fellow human being, then surely I can at least try and remember your name.
Easier said than done ?

Not at all !

Let me first identify the reasons as to why we forget someone's name. Gentlemen, you meet a physically very attractive lady. She tells you her name. Are you looking into her eyes or at her breasts ? Ladies, I know you're laughing, but you do the same. When you meet a cute guy, have you honestly never looked at how tight his butt is ?

79

Maybe you are not the physical type, maybe when you meet someone for the first time you are thinking about how much commission they are worth to you, or the meeting you have to go to later. The bottom line, why we do not remember someone's name, is because we are not concentrating. That's it, no argument.

Our minds are too active. When you meet someone for the first time – STOP !

Look at the person **in the eyes** and ask them their name.

1. Hear them say their name.
2. Repeat the name to make sure you got it right and that they heard that you got it right.
3. Now ask them something about their name. Is it short for something ? Where does it come from ? How do you spell it ?

This process is very important. You must force yourself to hear their name at least 3 times. By forcing yourself to do this you force yourself not to think of anything else. Don't you agree that the chances of you remembering their name is so much improved !

 And if it is a person from a different nation or culture, just ask more. Ask them to pronounce the name phonetically if you have difficulty understanding it. If I respect you as a fellow human being I will stand for half an hour trying to remember and pronounce your name and if you respect me as well you will appreciate my efforts and enthusiastically help me along !

Now take this even further and backtrack to remembering 5 things when entering a new office, room or shop. Apply this to the people you meet !

Look into a crowd, look at the people in your office pool, look at delegates attending a lecture. As you scan across the people there you will notice that one thing is unique to each person. It could be what they are wearing, their physical make, up, their race, whatever. If you were to walk away and come back again, it would be those same things that would strike you as unique about that individual again.

That's the first thing you focus on when meeting someone new. Again, it will take a few days to get used to doing this. Then over a period of three weeks build it up to instantly remembering 5 things about every person you meet. You have ample time to do this while you are approaching them and repeating their name three times. It may be awkward at first, but becomes completely natural after three weeks.

Let me pose an intriguing question to you.

Have you ever noticed that when you meet a really attractive person (someone that makes your heart beat faster) for the first time, it is very easy to remember their name ? And it is just as easy to remember all sorts of other things about them ... what they were wearing, the colour of their eyes, specific gestures they make, etc.

Why is this ?

Well, it's because you have shown more than a casual interest and have taken note of certain physical factors which have been part of the attraction. In other words, you have remembered more things than usual about this person because you were concentrating more than usual ! Same concept applies here.

In business, one of the biggest assets you as an individual can have, is the ability to remember clients names more easily. By using this method, you will dramatically increase the chance of remembering someone's name, and the next time you see them, you could even remember what they wore during the last meeting ! Imagine saying to a new client whom you have only met once before, for a short time, "That was a great suede jacket you had on at our last meeting Susan !"

How would you feel if someone you had met only once, remembered your name and what you wore on the last meeting ? It is so easy to do ! And suddenly you are giving personal attention to clients and noticing things no one else notices about them. Suddenly your client is no longer just a number, but someone who feel special. Who are they going to come back to for business ?

Makes you think !

Lastly, use the 5 item method while driving and practice defensive driving. How many accidents occur because drivers didn't see the car hitting them from the side, or the 2nd car ahead of them suddenly swerve to the right ?

Again, by trying to take note of 5 vehicles around you and what they are doing, you begin to drive defensively and safer. Alternatively, it reminds me of a cute line :

> *"Nothing improves your driving ...*
> *like a traffic cop driving behind you !"*

Don't let this be the case, make that traffic officer's job easier by driving defensively ! It could not only save your life, but the lives of those around you. How much effort does it really take to notice the two cars in front, the car on either side, and the car behind you ?

I was caught by a speed camera the other day and the traffic officer jumped into the road in front of my car, so quickly, that I only just managed to stop in time without knocking him over. You know what I mean ! As my car screeched to a halt he motioned to me to let down my driver side window. He stuck his head inside my car and shouted at me, "I've been waiting for you all day !" So I politely replied, "I came as fast as I could !"

They caught a friend of mine (Jacques) recently who is a juggler and he was returning home late one night from a show. His speciality is juggling with huge kitchen knives which he keeps on the back seat of his car. As the traffic officer pulled him over and began writing the ticket, he noticed the knives at the back and immediately quizzed Jacques about them. No matter how hard Jacques tried to explain, the officer wouldn't believe that he was a juggler.

Eventually Jacques had to get out of the car and juggle along the side of the highway. Now apparently at exactly the same time another car drove by with a couple inside who saw Jacques juggling his knives next to the highway with the traffic officer watching. The husband, eyes wide, suddenly turned to his wife and said, "Man I am glad I stopped drinking and driving, look at the tests they make you do now !"

I don't know why these stories are so funny. It must have something to do with the fact that we can all visualise these situations and really relate to them.

Here's another gem :

During a morning breakfast radio show the announcer interrupted a song with a news flash that there was a vehicle travelling on the wrong side of the highway towards oncoming traffic. A woman who heard this news flash knew that her husband, who was short sighted, was in and about that area at that moment. So she phoned him on his mobile phone and warned, "Herman, I just heard on the radio that there is a car travelling the wrong way down the highway and it's coming toward you !" To which Herman replied, "One !!! There are hundreds of them !"

You see – it's all about awareness !

A PIECE OF CAKE *by Author Unknown*

Sometimes we wonder, "What did I do to deserve this," or, "Why did 'the powers that be' have to do this to me." Here is a wonderful explanation !

A daughter is telling her Mother how everything is going wrong, she's failing algebra, her boyfriend broke up with her and her best friend is moving away. Meanwhile, her Mother is baking a cake and asks her daughter if she would like a snack, and the daughter says, "Absolutely Mom, I love your cake."

"Here, have some cooking oil," her Mother offers.

"Yuck" says her daughter.

"How about a couple raw eggs ?"

"Gross, Mom !"

"Would you like some flour then, or maybe baking soda ?"

"Mom, those are all yucky !"

DISCOVER YOUR MAGIC

To which the Mother replies: "Yes, all those things seem bad all by themselves. But when they are put together in the right way, they make a wonderfully delicious cake !"

Life works the same way. Many times we wonder why we must go through bad and difficult times.

This all builds character and make you a better person, and teaches you to appreciate the things we tend to take for granted such as the flowers every spring and a sunrise every morning. I hope your day is a "piece of cake !"

I cannot resist another great lesson.

MOMENTS IN LIFE by Author Unknown

There are moments in life when you miss someone so much that you just want to pick them from your dreams and hug them for real !

When the door of happiness closes, another opens; but often times we look so long at the closed door that we don't see the one, which has been opened for us.

Don't go for looks; they can deceive. Don't go for wealth; even that fades away. Go for someone who makes you smile, because it takes only a smile to make a dark day seem bright. Find the one that makes your heart smile.

Dream what you want to dream; go where you want to go; be what you want to be, because you have only one life and one chance to do all the things you want to do.

May you have enough happiness to make you sweet, enough trials to make you strong, enough sorrow to keep you human and enough hope to make you happy.

The happiest of people don't necessarily have the best of everything; they just make the most of everything that comes along their way.

The brightest future will always be based on a forgotten past; you can't go forward in life until you let go of your past failures and heartaches.

When you were born, you were crying and everyone around you was smiling. Live your life so at the end, you're the one who is smiling and everyone around you is crying.

Accept that some days you're the pigeon, and other days you're the statue.

Keep your words soft and sweet, in case you have to eat them.

Always read stuff that will make you look good if you die in the middle of it.

If you can't be kind, at least have the decency to be vague.

If you lend someone $50, and never see that person again, it was probably worth it.

Never put both feet in your mouth at the same time, because then you don't have a leg to stand on.

Nobody cares if you can't dance well. Just get up and dance.

Birthdays are good for you; the more you have, the longer you live.

DISCOVER YOUR MAGIC

You may be only one person in the world, but you may also be the world to one person.

Don't cry because it's over; smile because it happened.

A truly happy person is one who can enjoy the scenery on a detour.

Happiness comes through doors you didn't even know you left open.

In conclusion, to become more aware :

Understand what wealth is
Learn to love
Take note of conditioning
Become aware of the earth's energies

Remember 5 things about :
…..your surroundings
…...people you meet
…..while driving

And finally in this chapter, to quote one of the great motivational speakers of our time :

"I discovered a long time ago that if I helped people get what they wanted, I would always get what I wanted and I would never have to worry."

Zig Ziglar

Without looking up, or around ! Try and write down five things you can specifically remember, in the room in which you are sitting right now.

1.

2.

3.

4.

5.

Now let's make it slightly more difficult ! Try and write down five specific features you noticed about someone new, that you have met today.

1.

2.

3.

4.

5.

It isn't that easy, is it ?
Just by trying to do this here and now, you will have realised just how difficult it is ! Now you know for yourself how much time you need to spend on this exercise.

> *"It is those people that are aware,*
> *that discover all the opportunities in life first !"*
> **Wolfgang Riebe**

Notes

G = GOALS

Here are some more questions...

Have you ever dreamt of winning the lottery ?
Do you already know what you are going to do
with the cash when you do ?

Have you ever fantasised (let me finish...) of finding an
Aladdin's lamp, rubbing it and a genii appears who grants you 3
wishes ?
.... and you already know what your three wishes are ?

I have some news for you .... You do not have to win the lottery,
nor do you have to find an Aladdin's lamp !

Everything you desire in life you can have. Everything you need
to accomplish all of your dreams, you have on you right now.

Pretty bold statements huh ?

How often have you made a New year's resolution on old year's
eve ? e.g. "I am going to stop smoking as from tomorrow !"
Three weeks later you are smoking more than ever ! Apparently,
I am led to believe that 27 January is 'International Suicide Day'.
Why ? Well, by then everyone has realised that they won't stick
to their New Years resolutions, so what the hell !

Okay, let's backtrack. Most people do not achieve their dreams in life and this is a very depressing thought. Why is this so ? How come they give up on their dreams ? Numerous studies have been done and many complex theories and conclusions have come to the fore.

I laugh when I read most of them, never mind understanding them. So what's the answer ? Why don't we achieve our goals ?

Easy …. Because you don't believe you can !

It's easy to blame you peers, family and friends for not believing in you and influencing you. That's the easy way out.

How often have you heard people say that if you want something passionately enough you will achieve it ? Why is it that certain people actually do achieve their dreams and exceed them ?

Why could I, as a magician see the world, love what I do, get paid to do it, be the star of many of my own TV shows and still achieve more dreams every day ?

We are all the same, so what makes me different ? Was I part of the lucky sperm packet in life ? Did I know the right people ? Was I born with a gift ?

No !

All I did is what every human being on this earth can do. I believed in myself without letting outside influences distract me.

The first thing you must do is believe in yourself. If you, within your subconscious mind believe that you can do something, then nobody can make you think otherwise ! However, if your dreams are only superficial, fleeting desires with no depth, then you will be easily influenced.

91

"If you can dream it, you can achieve it", is not quite correct. It should be, "If you can dream it and **internalise** it, only then can you achieve it."

Why do we find it so difficult to get rid of bad habits, even though we know they are bad ? It's because they are embedded in our subconscious minds. Remember the hatred thorn ? Same concept.

What you have to do is create a desire thorn (not a hate thorn) inside your subconscious which grips tighter and tighter every day and never releases. Once your subconscious mind believes you can do something, then nothing will get in the way. The problem that arises is - how to get this seed thought embedded into your subconscious, that it stays there !

Now hold this thought while I ask you another question.
Do you agree that a goal would be, **"I want a new car !"** or **"I want a new house !"**

Is this a goal – yes or no ?

If you answered "Yes", which most people do, then you are wrong !
"I want a new car" is NOT a goal !

"I want a new Mercedes Benz C220 compressor. Elegance model with black leather interior and cherry wood finish. It must be tip-tronic with a sunroof, car kit, mag wheels and silver outside. I want this car in 6 months time and I am going to reach a specific business goal, of which I will save a certain amount of money per month." Now that's a goal !

See the difference ? One goal is broad and not detailed, the other is **specific**. Wanting a new house means nothing. Wanting a new house in Beverly Hills in LA, with 5 bedrooms, each with en suite and a triple garage. The street name, the size of the plot, the colour of the outside walls, the inside finishes, the time period in which you want to achieve this. This is a goal ! You need to specify everything exactly !

A goal is something that you desire so deeply, that you can experience it with your five senses, before you have it. It is this process which eventually assists you in attaining your goal.

Oscar Hammerstein once said :

> *"If you don't have a dream,*
> *how are you going to make a dream come true ?"*

Richard Bach put it so nicely :

> *"You are never given a dream,*
> *without also being given the power to make it true."*

How do you make that dream come true ?

First of all you need to BELIEVE you can achieve your dream. The only way you can accomplish this is by making your subconscious mind believe you can do it. And guess what, there is a simple way to do this.

Take your goal and write it down **specifically**, read it out **aloud** and **visualise** it using your **five senses.** Do this 3 times per day. Stick this list next to your bed and read it when you wake up. Stick another copy behind your desk and read this at lunchtime.

Finally before going to sleep, read the list one final time.

> **Repeat this everyday for 3 weeks and your mind will no longer distinguish between what is real and not !**

Here ! That 3 week scenario comes in again ! After doing this religiously for 3 weeks, this thought will have imbedded itself into your subconscious mind. This is when you, from within yourself, will start believing. You have now created a subconscious 'Seed Thought/Belief'. It is only when you **believe** that you will have the determination to go out and achieve the goal.

I'll never forget when I got to London the first time. No home, no friends, no money. My number one goal was that I would appear on BBC television. I wrote down this goal specifically with details as to how long it would take, how it would feel, what I would have to do, etc. Naturally all based on what I imagined it would be like. Every time I read my goal I could hear the audience clap, I could smell the inside of the studio, I could feel the warmth of the studio lights on me, I could taste the excitement in my mouth, I could see myself standing in the limelight.

I cannot over emphasise the importance of using ALL 5 SENSES when you visualise. Leaving one out will ruin everything. YOU MUST use all 5 senses !

I remember going to so many auditions in London that eventually I thought my name was, "**Next** !" I walked those streets for 2 years never giving up. What was it that gave me that determination ? It was my internal belief that I was going to make it. I believed ! Thus, every time I went to an audition and was turned down, I never saw it as a negative. Instead I saw it as one "No" closer to the final 'Yes'. The only reason I could do this was because my mindset had changed. I would have walked the streets for 4 years if I had to. The bottom line is that I practised the technique of getting my goals into my subconscious mind as seed thoughts and once this had been done, nobody, but nobody could change my mind !

Think back and ask yourself why you have not achieved all your goals ? You stopped dreaming, you gave up. No one said that it is easy, and there definitely will be hurdles. But if you don't believe in yourself then these hurdles become huge obstacles which throw you off course. However, if you do believe in yourself, these hurdles just make you stronger !

That's quite a statement for me to make and I would like to prove to you that this really works. Read the exercise below, concentrate and visualise everything that I describe to you.

> *I want you to imagine that you are walking into your kitchen towards the refrigerator. You now grab the handle and pull open the door. Feel the cold air rushing out onto your body. You now reach inside, and pick up a big, fresh, cold, ripe, yellow lemon. Squeeze it, and feel its coldness and rippled skin. Bring it up to your nose and smell its freshness. Now close the refrigerator door, and move towards the drawer that contains all the sharp knives. Open the drawer, and as you do this, you can hear the slight rattle of the knives inside.*
>
> *Look inside, and remove the sharpest knife. Now slowly cut the lemon in half. Feel the juice running down your hand, as you cut through the lemon. In fact, you have a small cut on your middle finger, and can feel the lemon juice burn you slightly. Once you have cut the lemon in half, place the knife aside on the counter. Now separate the two halves of the lemon, so that you have one half in each hand.*
>
> *Lastly, bring one half up to your nose, and again, take a deep breath, and smell that fresh lemon smell. Now open your mouth, place the half into your mouth and bite deep into the lemon !*

DISCOVER YOUR MAGIC

A question :

Do you now suddenly have an excess of saliva in your mouth after reading the above ?

I am 100% positive that you do !

Why is this ?

Simple ! You imagined the above example using all 5 of your senses. Hence you deceived your brain and sent a message to your subconscious mind that you really did bite into a lemon and hence your body increased your saliva excretion to compensate for the sour lemon.

Now ! Exactly the same applies to your goals. If you imagine them like this every day – your mind will believe that they exist before they really do.

In other words, your mind will believe what you desire, and hence you will act in accordance with this believe and logically and naturally put in that extra effort to achieve your goal.

As **Henry Ford** put it :

> *"Whether you think you can or think you can't,*
> *you are right."*

Many years ago, **Aristotle** already new this when he said :

> *"We are what we repeatedly do.*
> *Excellence is therefore not an act, but a habit."*

As a child I used to imagine myself standing on a famous stage in England, performing to a big audience. I could see the stage in my mind's eye. I could smell the old mustiness and hear the audience cheering. I felt the cards in my hands as I amazed the audience and tasted the saltiness of the sweat running down my forehead with excitement.

When I stood on the Leeds City Varieties stage in 1990 (where Charlie Chaplin and the 3 Stooges had all appeared), I knew the world was at my feet and anything was possible.

Leeds City Varieties Theatre : UK

So whatever your dream, visualise it specifically and believe – and you can have anything you want !

Do not just limit this to materialistic goals ! What about personal growth ? I want to be more positive or I want to be friendlier to my staff around me. This works for everything in life.

I remember having a huge problem saying 'Yes' and 'No'. Often someone would ask me to do something which I either didn't want to do or didn't have the time to do it. Yet I always felt obliged to say 'Yes'. Then I would kick myself afterwards that I did not say 'No'. Sound familiar ?

How did I overcome this ?

DISCOVER YOUR MAGIC

Easy, I applied the above principal. However, there is one problem ... and this has to do with using all 5 senses. How can I imagine myself being confident enough to say 'Yes' and 'No' and imagine this using all 5 of my senses ? How do I include the sense of smell into this scenario ?

If you find yourself in a situation where this is indeed the case ... FORCE IT ! Let me explain. I imagined myself saying 'Yes' and 'No' to someone while standing in front of a coffee machine. Hence I forced the coffee aroma into the whole scenario.

If you don't believe me, try for yourself. Attempt visualising a goal with only 4 senses. You will see that it doesn't work and your internal belief is not there.

> **It's all 5 senses or nothing !**

I have also found that many people have difficulty in coping with work loads and getting everything done in the office. Their goals are just to get through the day !

How can you alleviate stress and make your daily work routine more efficient and easier using goal setting techniques ?

Most of us have a pile of work to go through and don't know where to start. This alone causes delays and wastes time.

Take all your tasks for the month and prioritise them. In other words, if you have 20 things to do, look at each one and give each a number from 1 to 3. 1 has to be done right now, 2 can be done tomorrow, and 3 can wait a while. Put all the 1's on top of your list, followed by the 2's and then the 3's. The five minutes it takes you to make up this list will save you hours in the long run.

Expand on this concept with your own goals. If you have one large goal such as buying a new home in 3 years time, create a flow chart.

Set up the main goal in No. 1 position, for 3 years. Now create 3 blocks underneath the main goal, each representing one year. Now go to each year and divide it up into 12 months and write down what you need to achieve in each of those months. Go back to each month and divide them into 4 weeks and make weekly goals. You have now created a flow chart with logical simplified smaller goals all building up to the final goal.

Often we only have the bigger picture in mind and this clouds our train of thought. Many people do not realise that it is the combination and achievement of all the smaller goals that eventually lead to the final goal.

Let me simplify it even more. Assume you want to buy a holiday home in 2 years time. That's the goal. However, there is a lot of planning and research that goes into achieving this goal.

Where do you want to buy the holiday home ? What price do you want to pay ? These are all mini goals you need to complete before you can actually buy the home.

Hence, the first two months you set yourself the goal of just finding the right area. The next two months you set yourself the goal of researching various prices in the area of homes. And so you go on.

99

In this instance, the purchase of the holiday home is only the final small fraction of work involved in achieving that goal. So if you only see the goal of buying the home in two years as the be all and end all – it won't work. Hence by breaking down the goal into smaller mini goals you give everything a structured order and hence will feel as if you have achieved something towards the final goal.

If you don't do this, you may have spent 18 months researching and running around to buy the house, but because that 'buying of the house' is the final picture, you experience frustration as you haven't achieved it yet. But by breaking it down with mini goals you will realise after 18 months that you have done 99% of the work already to achieve it. Hence the final buying of the house is simply a formality.

Naturally all the goals you set need to be realistic and achievable. Do not try to overtax yourself. Rather put down less weekly goals and achieve extra ones if you have the time. If you cannot complete all in one week, carry these over to the next week and begin with them.

Can you recall everything you achieved last month, or last year ? I have found in my life, that if I write down everything I have to do on a list, and it sits on my desk everyday – it motivates me to take action. If I just live my life day by day and not write down any goals, I never seem to achieve anything I want to, and never have enough time for anything.

Remember we are a visual species. If you have a list on your desk and cross off everything as you have done it, at the end of the day or week you are giving your achievements an added visual confirmation which in turn again inspires you to do more.

If after a month or even a year you go back to your goal lists and see what you have achieved in this period, you will be pleasantly surprised to see just how much you are capable of. The well known & respected speaker, Zig Ziglar put this into really nice perspective when he said :

> *"What you get by achieving your goals is not as important as what you become by achieving your goals."*

> *"There are some people who live in a dream world, and there are some who face reality; and then there are those who turn one into the other."*
> **Douglas Everett**

> *"Ordinary people believe only in the possible. Extraordinary people visualize not what is possible or probable, but rather what is impossible. And by visualizing the impossible, they begin to see it as possible."*
> **Cherie Carter-Scott**

In summary, to make your dreams come true :

> **Write them down**
> **Be specific**
> **Read them aloud every day**
> **Visualize them using your 5 senses, and**
> **Break them down into small sub goals**

DISCOVER YOUR MAGIC

Notes

DISCOVER YOUR MAGIC

I = IMPRESSIONS

 I would like to start this chapter with another story by an unknown author which brilliantly portrays the power of impressions.

THE HOSPITAL WINDOW

Two men, both seriously ill, occupied the same hospital room. One man was allowed to sit up in his bed for an hour each afternoon to help drain the fluid from his lungs. His bed was next to the room's only window. The other man had to spend all his time flat on his back. The men talked for hours on end. They spoke of their wives and families, their homes, their jobs, their involvement in the military service, where they had been on vacation.

Every afternoon when the man in the bed by the window could sit up, he would pass the time by describing to his roommate all the things he could see outside the window. The man in the other bed began to live for those one-hour periods where his world would be broadened and enlivened by all the activity and color of the world outside. The window overlooked a park with a lovely lake. Ducks and swans played on the water while children sailed their model boats. Young lovers walked arm in arm amidst flowers of every color and a fine view of the city skyline could be seen in the distance.

103

As the man by the window described all this in exquisite detail, the man on the other side of the room would close his eyes and imagine the picturesque scene.

One warm afternoon the man by the window described a parade passing by. Although the other man couldn't hear the band - he could see it in his mind's eye, as the gentleman by the window portrayed it with descriptive words.

Days and weeks passed.

One morning, the day nurse arrived to bring water for their baths only to find the lifeless body of the man by the window, who had died peacefully in his sleep. She was saddened and called the hospital attendants to take the body away.

As soon as it seemed appropriate, the other man asked if he could be moved next to the window. The nurse was happy to make the switch, and after making sure he was comfortable, she left him alone.

Slowly, painfully, he propped himself up on one elbow to take his first look at the real world outside. He strained to slowly turn to look out the window beside the bed.

It faced a blank wall. The man asked the nurse what could have compelled his deceased roommate who had described such wonderful things outside this window.

The nurse responded that the man was blind and could not even see the wall.

She said, "Perhaps he just wanted to encourage you."

 *Recently I was performing and emceeing in New York at an awards evening. In-between the formalities and my performance they had a band playing dance music. As I was there for the whole night I thought it opportune to ask one of the ladies for a dance.*

However, the music was so loud, it was difficult to speak or even shout at anyone. Communication was pretty much limited to hand signals. I didn't realise it at the time, but one of the ladies had arrived late and didn't know who I was. It just so happened, that I caught her eye as she sat down and I mimicked to her if she would like to dance.

After ten minutes on the dance floor I was becoming quite hot as it was a black tie function, and my silk tuxedo didn't breathe very well. I needed to cool down and have a drink. Again I couldn't shout at the lady, as this would have been rude. So while dancing I again mimicked to her whether we should move to the bar for a drink.

As we arrived at the bar, another man appeared out of nowhere and shouted to this lady, "Hey Shirley, do you want to dance ?" To whom she shouted back, "No, I'm stuck with this deaf and dumb guy !"

Yep ! First impressions can be deceptive !

Once you have mastered the lesson in awareness, your first impression of people will become much more accurate than before. In today's society, first impressions play a big role, and can make or break a deal for you.

So often people are caught out, as first impressions can be wrong. In this chapter I want to highlight a few points which I believe will make you so much more perceptive.

One cold rainy night, a couple is sleeping. Suddenly there is a knock on the door at 3 am in the morning. Jumping up, the husband runs downstairs to find a drunk standing at the door. "Can you give me a push ?" the drunk asks. Totally annoyed, the husband slams the door shut and stomps back upstairs.

Pulling the duvet over him aggressively, the wife asks, "What's wrong honey ?" He snaps back ! "That was a stupid drunk at the door who wanted a push. Can you believe it ? Three am in the morning ! The cheek of it !"

The wife calmly smiles, replying, "Remember two weeks ago when your car broke down ? If it wasn't for those two chaps that gave you a push, you would have been stuck on the highway all night." And makes her husband feel guilty.

Feeling bad and agreeing that he may have over reacted, he gets up, puts on some warm clothes, and makes his way downstairs. Opening the front door, the howling wind and rain sprays into his face, but he cannot see the drunk anywhere. Walking outside to the front gate, he still cannot see the drunk.

He shouts, "Are you still there ?"
In the distance he softly hears, "Yesh."
"Do you still need a push ?" he shouts.
Again the drunk replies, "Yesh."
This time the man shouts, "Where are you ?"
Eventually the drunk replies, "Here ! By the swing !"

When I read this joke for the first time, I couldn't stop laughing, and it kind of portrays exactly what I am trying to say … first impressions can be deceptive. That's also the success and the humour in this joke. It totally deceives you by leading you in a completely wrong direction, and the unexpected, yet obvious punch line is what makes the whole thing so funny.

Yes ! People are still very body conscious, especially being exposed to all the so-called beautiful people in the media. However, a growing awareness is coming to the fore that you cannot judge people merely by their physical appearance alone.

For many people this is a new and confusing concept and they need to learn what to look for in others.

Do you know which part of the human body is the most revealing ?

Many people think it is the eyes. Yes ! An Iridologist can tell you lots of interesting things about illnesses you have had, just by looking at your eyes. However, this is something that 99.9% of the population cannot do, as it needs intensive study and instruments to look into the eye. I mean, imagine meeting someone for the first time and saying, "Excuse me, just sit down here for a moment while I examine your eyes!"

The most revealing part of the human body is the **hands** ! Think about this for a moment. The first time your meet someone and see that they have dirty hands … what does it tell you about that person ?

An attractive, well dressed woman sits in your office for an interview. However, you notice that her nail polish is chipped and unkempt. What does this tell you ?

You are at a meeting discussing a new product your company wants to purchase. The man opposite you has finger nails which have been bitten to shreds.

What does this tell you ?

Without a doubt, your hands can give away many facts about yourself. Remember the classic movie, "Gone with the Wind" where the heroine, Scarlet O'Hara wanted to impress the leading man in the film ? She dressed herself to the hilt, got the proper English accent down pat. She pulled it off perfectly, except for one thing. Her hands gave her away ! As they were the hands someone who did a lot of cleaning and manual work.

Ladies still tend to end up doing the dishes most of the time. How often have you heard them comment that the dish wash makes their hands look old ? Gentleman, look at the hands of every woman you meet. You can almost always bet that those with really well kept hands own a dish washer, have a maid, and have husbands that really pamper them.

Ladies, when you see a man with grimy finger nails, and well worn hands, you can again almost always bet that he is in the motor mechanic trade, or something similar.

So do yourself a favour and study the hands of everyone you know and see how they fit together.

Just as a throw-in, do you know what the 2nd most revealing part of the human body is ?

The heel of the foot !

Bet that caught you ! Why ? Consider the Middle East where everyone wears kaftans and the women's faces are covered. The only way you can tell their age or get to know anything about them is by looking at the heels of their feet!

To improve your chances in making the correct first impression, **focus like a laser**. To bring this point into perspective I would like to ask you whether you are guilty of, or have experienced the following situation.

 You are at a cocktail party, or business function. The host of the party (could be you) speaks to you and suddenly asks you a question which is very close to your heart. As you start answering, he/she turns around to speak to another guest who has come into the conversation. When the host is eventually finished with this person, he/she turns their attention back to you and has completely forgotten what they asked you earlier on.

If this has happened to you – what do you think of that host ? I dare to say, your first impression will be that that person is an insincere schmuck ! And you will be correct. Should you have been guilty of this behaviour yourself, it is time that you changed your approach, as your peers, and possible new contacts will most likely also see you as an insincere schmuck !

This is where focusing like a laser plays a role. In the chapter dealing with awareness I said that you should remember 5 points about others. Once you have mastered this you'll notice that you automatically start focusing like a laser. However, it's no use only doing this momentarily in order to gain the information you need. Your concentration should always be 100%.

Yes I know that hosting a cocktail or business function demands that your eyes and ears are everywhere. However, let us look at the situation again. A stranger has been introduced to you. There is nobody else around and you start chatting. Firstly, **show a genuine interest** in this person so that when you ask a question, it is something you genuinely want to know. This together with **focusing your attention** will make it natural for you to remember what you are asking.

If at this point someone else wants to join in the conversation, they are INTERRUPTING you ! They can either wait until you

DISCOVER YOUR MAGIC

have finished, which is rare. Mostly they just interrupt your conversation. Thus you are fully entitled to momentarily turn to them and say, "Just give me a minute so that I can finish off here."

Then you turn back to your original guest and apologise for the interruption, and excuse yourself, saying that you would really enjoy finishing your conversation at a later point in time, and hope that he/she can understand that everyone wants your attention at this moment in time. Only now, do you turn to the 2nd person. And if the opportunity exists, make a point of going back to the original guest, and finish off your conversation.

What does this accomplish for you ? Firstly, your original guest doesn't feel insulted or left out. By explaining the predicament and finishing off the conversation, apologising and offering to carry on later, you have made a friend rather than an enemy. The 2nd person who tried to interrupt, also respects you for what you have done and sees your sincere interest in the other person. A win-win situation !

But it is only by focusing your attention and making a point of doing this that it will happen. It is so easy, yet so many people fail to do this. At the end of the day, it is all good and well to be motivated, but if you walk over others, that energy is not going to come back to you.

If you want to create a good impression, remembering a person's name is very important, but imagine if you could remember their birthday as well ?

It is only in the insurance industry that I have seen brokers and financial advisors send out birthday cards to their clients. Not many do this either.

Today's business world is so competitive, and wherever you can get the edge, you need to do so. Many companies advertise their services on a regular basis. As an example let us say that every 3 months you do a big advertising campaign.

Imagine that one of your clients has his/her birthday over this period. Now instead of advertising, you send this person a personalised birthday card. No business, just a normal card bought from a store which you signed in your own handwriting. Maybe a comment such as, *"I remembered it was your birthday today and wanted to wish you much health and happiness in the coming year."*

How do you think that client will react ? Yes, they may be surprise. But I can almost guarantee that they will feel good and touched that you remembered their birthday. So what does this bring you ?

Just think one step further. You have crossed the boundary between business and personal friendship. This client suddenly feels that he/she is more than just a business contact. The next time he/she needs products or services related to your business, who do you think they will go to ? What is more, they will tell their friends and other business associates about the extra service you give. The cherry on top is that you can achieve this without sending any marketing or advertising material.

Makes you think ! Okay, I hear you say, "How do I get hold of their birth date ?" Easy ! Early on in this chapter I told you to focus like a laser.

Why ? Because other people don't !

So, in your initial conversation you could easily make a comment such as, "Aren't you a Gemini ?" If they are, you will have created a brilliant impression. If they aren't, no problem. Either way, this comment allows you to say, "So what star sign are you ? Aah, and what day ?"

There you have it. Because this was done in a so-called casual manner, that person won't even realise you have taken note of their birth date. Hence it is a must that you keep a pen & notebook with you at all times so that you can go off and jot this down.

 Sending a birthday card is great and personal, but phoning is much BETTER. Much more personal, and cheaper. And more than likely, if you phone and give your birthday wishes, this client will turn the conversation to business himself and maybe even place an order !

Recently I mentioned this whole birthday issue to someone and they thought they were clever by saying, "But what if I have 500 clients who have a birthday in one day ?" Highly unlikely, but even here the answer to this is simple ………….. Email !

One email and everyone receives their birthday wish. Aah ! "But this is not personal, I hear you say !" Email is a very powerful medium and as such you could attach a personally recorded voice message, which will then give it that 'personal' feel. See – there's a solution for everything !

Now I have to share, what I believe to be one of my classic experiences and boldest moves ever, on the subject of creating the right impression ! When I started out in the UK I was really down and out, sharing a bed-sit with 3 other people. It was tough. Through a friend I received a contact name of a well known agent in London who was a 'go-getter' and only booked top acts.

One of his criteria when interviewing potential new acts, was to visit them in their homes to see just how successful they were and whether they were really as 'big' as most acts make themselves out to be.

112

I didn't know this. So I phoned him up and really laid it on thick about myself and my accomplishments and how good I was. It sounded as if he was duly impressed and he set up a meeting with me that day for 2 o'clock. I could feel the excitement building up within me. Then came the crash. He asked me for my address, as he wanted to come to my place.

What does one do in a situation like this ? I was sharing a 2 x 2 room with 3 other chaps, in a really bad area of London. To this date I don't know why I said this, but I suddenly blurted out that I was staying at the Hilton and would meet him there. As I put that phone down my heart was racing and I wanted to kick myself so hard.

Nevertheless I had about 4 hours to pull this off. I went down to a car hire place around the corner and asked to hire a C180 Mercedes (smallest one) for 5 hours. They wanted my credit card and driver's license. I only had £100 cash on me and offered £80. The clerk behind the desk wasn't interested, he wanted a credit card and I didn't have a credit card. As a down & out entertainer I was a bad credit risk for a bank anywhere. Here came my first obstacle, I couldn't hire the car for cash, I needed a credit card.

So I did what any proud male would do. Look the clerk in the eyes, and told him that I would take my business elsewhere ! I walked up and down the high streets – nobody would hire me a car without a credit card. Eventually I had to come up with another plan. To this day I don't know why I did this, but I went back up to my bed sit, packed all my tricks and belongings into the only two suitcases I owned, and went back down to the original car hire place.

You see, I had been living in this area for a while, and most people where familiar to me in the stores, and I to them. I walked past them every day going, to and from the tube station.

I looked the clerk in the eyes, put down my suitcases, took out my passport and any other documents I had and said to him, "Here's my passport, you know I live over there, here's my dad's address, my mom in law, my grandmother, my 2nd cousin removed, etc. etc. …. Please hire me the car !" To this day I don't know why, but he did. Maybe he saw how desperate I was, or maybe he was just a good person. I put down my £80 and he hired me the Mercedes !

At 13h55 I arrived at the entrance to the Hilton, stopped the car and left the engine running. I checked with the doorman whether I could leave the car running while I went inside to fetch a 'guest'. When I got inside the foyer was quiet, so I went to the receptionist and asked her if she would like to see a trick ?

What a lame come-on line !!!

Well, it worked, and she laughed as I fooled her. I then told her that my name was Wolfgang Riebe and I was here to meet an important entertainment agent. Should he come to the reception desk and ask for me, would she point him in my direction ? She was more than willing to do so, as I had shown her a trick and made her laugh.

I had about 2 minutes to wait, so I decided to take the elevator up to the 2nd floor to check how the wealthy live. Man that hotel had wide passages. Thereafter I took the elevator straight down again. Have you ever heard of the saying, "That Kodak moment." I had one that day !As the doors opened on the ground floor, I saw a man walking towards the reception desk.

It was the agent who inquired about my whereabouts. The receptionist immediately pointed to me, as I was exiting the elevator (talk about timing). This created the impression in the agent's mind, that I lived there. After all, the receptionist knew who I was !

We shook hands, made some small talk and I told him that I was sick of hotel food (I wish) and wanted to go have something small in one of the nearby parks. He agreed, we got into my hired Mercedes, and I took him for lunch, which cost me less than £10.

Needless to say, I got lots of work from this man by creating the right first impression ! I know my example is extreme, but I consider it to be one of those lucky perfect timing moments in my life !

Let's look at impressions from another perspective !
Think about your work colleagues. Whom do you find most intriguing ? Those who you know everything about, or those that have a bit of mystery around them ? As a magician, I have secrets and don't divulge them. There is something special and mysterious about me, and this makes me an interesting person. No one knows everything about me.

 If you meet someone for the first time, especially in a business environment, and you lay all your cards on the table – you have nothing left up your sleeve for further negotiations. It is the same when you meet someone and get on really well. You chat and tell your life history and cannot wait until you meet again. At the next meeting it isn't the same, you seem bored. Why ? Because you gave everything away at the first meeting.

If I want to make a business deal, I make sure that the prospective client is intrigued and interested by what I have to offer. I don't give out to much info on myself, thus keeping myself interesting !

Have you ever worked in a large office pool and someone has

gotten a promotion ? Think back. What kind of person this was ? Yes ! They would have been a good worker, but very likely they would have been someone interesting. Those that were up for the same promotion, and didn't get it – who were they ? Most likely people who everyone knew, but had nothing else to offer in terms of the mystery element.

Think about it, what attracted you to your current partner initially, besides the physical ? It was the mystery of the person ! What kept the interest, was the finding out of who they were. Hence many relationships die out, because the mystery is gone. So it should be your goal to continually surprise your partner and come up with something totally unexpected – this keeps the fire alive !

JUST AN "OLD LADY" ?

When an old lady died in the geriatric ward of a small hospital near Dundee, Scotland, it was believed that she had nothing left of any value. Later, when the nurses were going through her meagre possessions, they found this poem. Its quality and content so impressed the staff that copies were made and distributed to every nurse in the hospital.

One nurse took her copy to Ireland. The old lady's sole bequest has since appeared in the Christmas edition of the News Magazine of the North Ireland Association for Mental Health.

A slide presentation has also been made based on her simple, but eloquent, poem. And this little old Scottish lady, with nothing left to give to the world, is now the author of this 'anonymous' poem winging across the Internet.

CRABBY OLD WOMAN

What do you see, nurses ?

What do you see ?

What are you thinking when you're looking at me ?

A crabby old woman, not very wise, uncertain of habit with faraway eyes ? Who dribbles her food and makes no reply, when you say in a loud voice, "I do wish you'd try !" Who seems not to notice the things that you do, and forever is losing a stocking or shoe ? Who, resisting or not, lets you do as you will, with bathing and feeding, the long day to fill ?

Is that what you're thinking ? Is that what you see ? Then open your eyes, nurse, you're not looking at me. I'll tell you who I am as I sit here so still, as I do at your bidding, as I eat at your will. I'm a small child of ten with a father and mother, brothers and sisters, who love one another.

A young girl of sixteen with wings on her feet dreaming that soon now a lover she'll meet. A bride soon at twenty, my heart gives a leap, remembering the vows that I promised to keep. At twenty-five now, I have young of my own, who need me to guide and secure a happy home.

A woman of thirty, my young now grown fast, bound to each other with ties that should last. At forty, my young sons have grown and are gone, but my man's beside me to see I don't mourn.

At fifty once more, babies play round my knee, again we know children, my loved one and me.

Dark days are upon me, my husband is dead, I look at the future, I shudder with dread. For my young are all rearing young of their own, and I think of the years and the love that I've known. I'm now an old woman and nature is cruel; 'Tis jest to make old age look like a fool.

The body, it crumbles, grace and vigor depart, there is now a stone where I once had a heart. But inside this old carcass a young girl still dwells, and now and again, my battered heart swells. I remember the joys, I remember the pain, and I'm loving and living life over again. I think of the years all too few, gone too fast, and accept the stark fact that nothing can last.

So open your eyes, people, open and see, not a crabby old woman; look closer . . . see ME !!

Remember this poem when you next meet an old person who you might brush aside without looking at the young soul within .. . we will all, one day, be there, too !

In summary then :

First impressions can be deceptive
Focus like a laser
Always devote your full attention to others
Keep the mystery alive

Notes

C = CHANGE

> *"If we don't change, we don't grow. If we don't grow, we are not really living. Growth demands a temporary surrender of security. It may mean a giving up of familiar but limiting patterns, safe but unrewarding work, values no longer believed in, relationships that have lost their meaning. As Dostoevsky put it, 'Taking a new step, uttering a new word, is what people fear most.' The real fear should be of the opposite course."*
>
> **Gail Sheehy**

 Even though I am considered to be the 'Change Management Expert' and this chapter is titled, 'Change' - this whole book is about changing the way you see life and everything around you. Chris Rea sang a well known song called, "Highway to Hell". Few people realise he was writing about the M25 around London. It is the ring road around this city and all other roads in England join the M25 …. So you can imagine the traffic !

I recall sitting one morning in one of those jams, being totally irritated and knowing my day was off to a bad start. Suddenly, the chap in the car next to me held up a cardboard sign which said, "Hi, my name's George!"

I thought this was a cute idea, smiled and waved. Then he held up another sign which read, "Crappy weather today, don't you agree ?" This was followed by numerous other signs he had made. What George had done, was break the boredom of sitting in these traffic jams. Within about ten minutes of him showing his first sign, all the surrounding cars knew George and everyone was smiling.

George had managed to inject change into the morning's traffic jam ritual. No doubt to prevent himself from going crazy. I will never forget this day as it made me realise just how easy it is to fall into a rut and get pulled down by the everyday monotony of certain daily rituals life throws at us.

Let me pose some questions to you : How much of your life is routine ? Have you driven the same route to work for the past 6 months ? Is every Friday night the same for you ? Do you feel frustrated with your personal and work routine because nothing ever changes ?

If you answered, "Yes" to any of the above questions, my first suggestion is, **be open to change**. By this I mean that you simply need to accept the fact that your life cannot go on as it is at present, and that you need to add some change into your routine. Not big changes, **only small changes**. The object is to **smash the routine**, and build from there.

Some people are afraid of change and of making the choice to change. For those of you I have one comment. Even if you chose not to make the choice to change, you have still made a choice, so why not choose the change ?
As **Joe DiMaggio** said :

> *"If you keep thinking about what you want to do or what you hope will happen, you don't do it, and it won't happen."*

Most people believe this to be difficult to do. However, it is the easiest thing on earth. Just imagine that for as long as you can remember you have climbed out of the same side of bed, had the same waking up & breakfast routine.

Discover Your Magic

Tomorrow morning, why not get up from the opposite side of your bed ? (it could become quite interesting) Also, if you have always gone straight to the bathroom, don't do it now. Have a cup of coffee first. Basically mess up your normal routine. Do it in such a way that you won't lose any extra time, but that it just feels different.

If you have always driven to work via one route, use a different route tomorrow, even if you only drive left out of your driveway instead of right. The whole object of the exercise is to start with small changes.

Besides messing up your routine, what effect will this have on you ? First of all, when you get to work tomorrow you are going to feel different. Initially you won't be able to place your finger on it, but it will have to do with the slight change in your morning routine.

Even at work, if you always have coffee at a certain time, change to tea, or change the times. You will find that suddenly your day doesn't move at the slow speed it did before. Things will happen faster and seem more exciting.

The same goes for married couples who have become complacent with each other. They have been married for 10 years, and are bored. "My partner doesn't turn me on anymore. Sex isn't the same anymore." Have you ever considered, trying something completely different ? Don't wait until you get to bed exhausted before you try a feeble attempt to satisfy your partner.

Don't make the dishes and cleaning the house your priority and then be too tired to even try to spend some intimate time with your partner. That's the way most people do it – no wonder they are bored ! When you get home go for it on the kitchen table !

Buy the Kama Sutra – watch the DVD ! Send your partner shopping, or go with and make sure they buy clothes that they don't usually wear. Have your hair stylist create a new look you !

Do you know people in your work place that won't adapt to change ? I have seen it so often where people say, "I have always done it this way, why must I change ?" At the rate that technology is advancing, if you don't keep up, you will be left behind. Hence you must be open to change.

In 1993 and 1994 I worked on a cruise ship owned by Cunard, called the Vistafjord. It was considered to be one of the top ships in the world with a 5 star plus rating. The unique feature of this ship was that the passenger-compliment consisted of Americans, English and Germans. Hence every entertainer needed to speak both English & German fluently.

Being German, this was no problem for me. However, I worked mainly in the UK and had a British sense of humour which came across in my shows. On this ship though, we had 3 different cultures, and 3 different senses of humour. The British humour was clever, the American humour slapstick, and the Germans whose humour was very precise ! Also, most English jokes were not always possible to translate into German.

Performing on Cunard's m/s Vistafjord

123

I had to adapt and change my entire act to fit in with 3 different cultures. I believe I was the only act to work on this ship for such a long period of time. Nobody else lasted as long as I did.

Why ?

Because they didn't adapt their acts to fit the passengers. Their acts had worked everywhere else. Why should they change it now ? By me adapting my act and fitting in with the company's and passengers needs I secured myself record long contracts, made many great friends and learnt so much more about other people and myself.

Do you have a security guard at the entrance to your building ? What about a cleaning service or maid that cleans up during the day or in the evening ? If you take public transport to work, do you see the same faces every day ? If yes, do you know their names ? Tomorrow morning on your way to work, every person you have seen more than twice, whose name you don't know – go up to them and introduce yourself and talk to them !

In two days time when you go to work, guess what will happen? Suddenly people you only saw before and never knew, are going to smile at you and say, "Hello !" When you greet the security guard at the door, he will say, "Hello !" From going to work all glum and not smiling, you now have a whole new group of people to converse with.

Do you recall that earlier on, I mentioned the importance of remembering a name and how nice it is to hear your own name ? Suddenly you will have heard your own name numerous times, have had people smile at you, before you get to work. All of this you never had before !

Can you see the nice change that this will bring about in your frame of mind ?

 *A chap goes to the psychologist complaining that his marriage has become boring and that the spark is gone. The psychologist immediately suggests he break the routine by going to the florist, buying some flowers and surprising his wife at home with these. The man agrees that this is a good idea and visits the closest florist and buys a bunch of red roses.*

On his way home he decides he will surprise his wife by simply ringing the doorbell and not just walking into the house. On arrival he walks up the front garden path, rings the doorbell and patiently waits for his wife to answer. Eventually she comes to the door dressed in her night-gown. It is one of those chiffon green night-gowns with the fluffy frills around the edges. She has a half smoked cigarette in her mouth. Pink hair curlers in her hair. Light blue cloth slippers on, with the backs walked off.

She looks at her husband in surprise with the roses in his hand and says, " I don't believe it ! I just don't believe it ! The kids are sick. Your son just vomited all over his bed. The maid didn't pitch this morning. I had to clean the whole kitchen, including all the weekend's dishes. The vacuum cleaner broke. On top of that the dog dies and your daughter is in hysterics. And now you come home drunk !!!!!!"

A cute story, but very true ! How many of you would have the same reaction ? Would it surprise you if your partner suddenly came home with a gift for you ? When you met your partner the first time, one of the things that attracted you was that you didn't quite know what was going to happen next. There was an element of mystery. The same applies in your work environment. If you are forever changing (for the positive), and people don't get used to you as the same old so and so – you are far more respected.

You need to keep that change and mystery going, as I mentioned in the chapter on "Impressions".

DISCOVER YOUR MAGIC

A wonderful saying that I read many years ago suggests that in a storm, the branches on an old hard dry tree will snap from the wind, but a young, fresh pliable tree's branches will just bend to accommodate the wind and then snap back into their original position again.

I would like to end this chapter with a personal example which showed me what the word 'change' really meant.

As a magician I have always led my life with a philosophy :

"Life isn't always about being dealt a good hand of cards,
but playing a bad hand well !"

And here's a true life example.

In July of 1997 I was on an Arctic expedition, on an expedition cruise ship which had approximately 120 passengers on board. One morning, a few days into the cruise at breakfast, at around 08h05 we all felt a sudden bump. We were cruising in pack ice, so I didn't think much of it. Suddenly the Captain made an announcement that the ship has run aground.

m/s Hanseatic : Arctic Pack Ice

126

Of course everyone was up on deck and even though the ship had a small draught of 4.2 meters, we had hit a sand/gravel bank.

Luckily there was a very small boat in the area which came alongside about two hours later, took a tow line and assisted in attempting to pull us off the sand bank while the Captain put on the bow thrusters.

Nothing happened, except that the ship listed to around 11 degrees. Otherwise we didn't budge ! 11 Degrees may not mean much to you. Let me put it into perspective. This means that everything on the tables slid off. If you put a cup of coffee on the table, it would start sliding to one side. The photos below will put it nicely into perspective for you.

Aft view

Me Standing
'Straight'

It appeared as if we were stuck and had to send an emergency stress call to Spitzbergen (the northern most continent) for the Norwegian coast guard to assist in pulling us off the sand-bank.

Of course we had older passengers on board who were now presented with an added problem of having to walk with a ship lying at an 11 degree angle. We had to keep them busy and prevent panic. Keep in mind also that these elderly people were already slightly unstable on their feet, and if they fell and broke a hip, even though we had medical facilities, we did not have a hospital. Such injuries could potentially be fatal for them.

DISCOVER YOUR MAGIC

Having worked so long on ships, I knew how to keep them entertained and could suggest stuff to do with them as well. However, this was not the Caribbean ! The temperatures were in the minus 10 degrees and colder regions !

As this was a small ship with only two entertainers, and as I had experience of sailing in Alaska, Antarctic and the Arctic, I was part of the team on board to keep things running smoothly. Furthermore, due to the extreme northern position and the angle of the satellite, we had no telephonic communication, except for short wave transmissions a few hours per day.

Once the press got wind of this, helicopters with CNN cameras broadcast this world wide. Family members would be worrying what was happening, as no one on board could contact home.

Keeping up with the philosophy of being open to change and playing a bad hand well, we decided to make the most of the situation we were in. The ship wouldn't budge, and where we were, there wasn't much ice. We therefore decided to have a mini expedition, and get all 120 passengers onto the zodiacs.

Mini expedition on the Zodiacs

However, it wasn't just as easy as that ! Remember that these were unexplored waters, and walruses with big teeth could get annoyed if we came to close, and could rupture the zodiacs. Not

128

forgetting that the water was freezing cold, and no one would survive for more than a minute if any accidents occurred. We had to plan our zodiac trip carefully, and make sure we had rifles with us, in case we spot a walrus.

As fate would have it, we spotted a walrus. This could have been a potentially dangerous situation. Besides it attacking and eating the passengers, it could also attack the zodiac, causing it to sink. The chances of survival in the icy waters would be extremely slim.

The entire crew had experience in the Arctic. We had all sailed here for many years, and therefore knew the safe distance to keep, from the wild animals. By falling back onto experience, and being open to change ,we got as close as we could to this walrus, to let the passengers experience this animal in its natural surroundings. Yet still keeping one zodiac to one side. with a gun pointed at the walrus in case anything happened.

Walrus encounter while on Zodiacs

Thankfully the first day went smoothly and most passengers saw the whole thing as an adventure. Everyone on board had to change their whole outlook. The chefs had to attempt to cook in the kitchen like this. People had to walk more carefully and hold onto the railings. There were numerous new factors no one had ever thought of.

DISCOVER YOUR MAGIC

That night, everyone attempted to prop their beds up on one side so they could sleep level. On waking the next morning and getting out of bed, most people had forgotten that their beds were level, and the floor wasn't. What happened ? They misjudged and fell ! Our first casualties !

When we all looked outside, the ice had floated into the area where we were stranded. The ship was now surrounded by 4 meter thick pack ice !

Standing on 4m thick pack ice.

This meant that the coast guard couldn't get to us either. We were truly stuck. Well, I have never done so much magic in my life before ... and that at 11 degrees !

By the 3rd day we were pulling our hair out for ideas to keep everyone occupied and calm. Then we came up with an excellent idea. Let's have a barbecue at the back of the ship !

This will truly be novel and a never to be forgotten experience. Take note that the gangways are permanently fixed on the side of the ship. Therefore, we had to put a step ladder down the back. Again, as most people were elderly, it took four crew members to assist them down onto the ice.

Of course this could only be done once we had checked out the thickness of the ice and whether it was indeed safe. Being an

DISCOVER YOUR MAGIC

expedition ship, we had thermal diving suits. The navigation officer, who was qualified to do such dives, first checked where the safe areas were. We found a safe area, cordoned it off with the mooring ropes and kept the passengers from walking outside these areas.

Getting ready for the barbecue !

The victuals and barbecue equipment also had to be lowered down the back for our Arctic Barbecue ! Now an interesting feature of the Arctic is that it is inhabited by Polar Bears. These guys can smell food from around 100km away and can run at speeds of up to 60km per hour. Their hair is translucent so as to absorb maximum sunlight and warmth. This leads to a problem because it means that they blend in with the background. On snow they look more white, in water more blue, against a rocky background more brown. Hence you don't see them so well in the distance ! The fourth and final fact about polar bears is that they are the most aggressive mammals on the globe. They may look cuddly, but they will attack you whether they are hungry or not !

We now had to keep watch, without scaring the passengers, and had to have an immediate plan to get them back onto the ship as soon as possible, should we spot one.

What would have happened had we not been open to this way of thinking and planning ahead. ?

DISCOVER YOUR MAGIC

Take this even further, what would have happened had we not been rescued. Could we have all frozen to death ?

How's that for cold ?

I want you to try imagine for one moment being in a position where you are stuck out in the ice. The temperatures drop to below, minus 40 degrees Celsius. You cannot keep warm anymore and you realise that you have about 20 minutes left to live.

What would go on in you mind ?

If now is not opportune, make a time in the future and set your alarm for 20 minutes. Sit through these 20 minutes, imagining you will be dead when the alarm goes off. Not something we want to think about. But do it !

Will you be in a position to say, "Hey, I am ready. I have had a full life with no regrets. Take me now !"

To the literally hundreds of thousands of delegates I have posed this question, NOT ONE has put up their hand to say they have no regrets.

How often have you heard someone say, or even said to others,

"Live every moment as if it is your last !"

Each and everyone of us are aware of this, but who really practices this ? I meet people that tell me, "One day if I die." Hello ! There is no "If", it's "When" you die. It's the inevitable !

Have you made plans for this ? Have you spoken to your loved ones ? Is your 'Will' in place ? Have you planned properly so that you don't die intestate, and the government takes most of your money for estate duty ?

When last did you look your spouse, or children in the eyes ,and say "I love you" ? When it comes to being an optimist and only seeing the positive side of life – that's me. However, even if I just go down the road to the corner café, I always kiss my wife and girls good-bye. I don't know what's going to happen. This is called being a realist !

If you have had a quarrel with your spouse, do you go to sleep and carry on the fight over a few days ? Whether I am in the right or not, I will be man enough to turn around and say, "I'm sorry, I love you." Imagine you wake up the next morning after a fight and your spouse has passed on, how would you feel ?

These are all important factors to consider when speaking about change. We as human beings need to change our attitudes, care more, and be more forgiving of those around us.

Not discussing or preparing for the day you are gone is irresponsible. Playing a bad hand well is about preparing for the inevitable and making sure everyone is taken care of.

Consider my question about regrets again. If you die now, will you have regrets ? If you answered affirmative to this then it's time you began changing your life and start living.

Take my life, so far everyone tells me how lucky I have been to see the world. Luck had nothing to do with it. I didn't want to work my whole life with the hope of being able to travel when I retire. And then, either be ill, frail or dead.

Today I can honestly sit back and say I fulfilled my dreams. Everything new that happens to me now is a bonus. It doesn't matter whether you succeed or fail. What matters is that you tried, and are able to look back, and know you gave it your best shot.

Back to my arctic adventure ...imagine if we hadn't been open to change and hadn't taken all the possibilities into account, and actually changed our way of thinking to fit in with our circumstances – do you think we would have survived ?

We sat it out for ten days before the ice thawed out. The coast guard arrived, and managed to pull us off after 17 hours. It was an adventure I will never forget, and a life lesson that made me realise the importance of change !

Coast Guard alongside

m/s Hanseatic being pulled free.

DISCOVER YOUR MAGIC

DAILY SURVIVAL KIT

Items needed : *Toothpick, Rubber Band, Band Aid, Pencil, Eraser, Chewing Gum, Mint, Candy Kiss, Tea Bag.*

WHY ?

TOOTHPICK
To remind you to pick out the good qualities in others.

RUBBER BAND
To remind you to be flexible, things might not always go the way you want, but it will work out.

BAND AID
To remind you to heal hurt feelings, yours or someone else's.

PENCIL
To remind you to list your blessing everyday.

ERASER
To remind you that everyone makes mistakes and it's OKAY.

CHEWING GUM
To remind you to stick with it and you can accomplish anything.

MINT
To remind you that you are worth a mint.

CANDY KISS
To remind you that everyone needs a kiss or a hug everyday

TEA BAG
To remind you to relax daily and go over that list of blessings

DISCOVER YOUR MAGIC

Now I want to share with you another lesson – how change affects others. It is by far the most profound story in this book. Most people who read it for the first time are completely shocked and in a daze ... but that's exactly the whole point of sharing it with you.

THE BLIND GIRL

There was a blind girl who hated herself because she was blind. In fact she hated everyone, except her loving boyfriend. He was always there for her and she promised him that if one day she could see the world, she would marry him.

Well, one day someone did donate a pair of eyes for her and as it turned out she could eventually see – even her boyfriend for the first time ! Of course he immediately asked her, "Now that you can see the world, will you marry me ?" The girl was shocked to see that her boyfriend was blind too, and therefore refused to marry him.

He walked away in tears, and later wrote her a letter saying:

"JUST TAKE CARE OF MY EYES PLEASE."

A friend of mine told me this story back in the early 90's and I have never forgotten it. This is so typical of how humans change when their circumstances change. Only a select few remember what their life was like before, and who were always there to support and comfort them in their painful situations. How many people do you know like this ?

One lesson I have learnt in life is to never forget where you came from and to ALWAYS be thankful for all the good things in your life. Every morning I open my eyes I am thankful for another day of health and a beautiful wife, plus two gorgeous daughters. Do you wake up thankful, or do you take everything for granted ?

I have pretty much given you my whole life story in this book, with it's ups and downs. Today I look back and will never forget the lessons life has thrown at me and how these have made me grow. They say that travelling is the 'University of Life' – well today I couldn't agree more !

In my industry egos are what it's all about. Once I had achieved my celebrity status with my TV shows, I will never forget the disappointment in being invited to 'so-called' status, high profile events and seeing how many people simply 'forget' where they came from. How people suddenly had respect for you because you were 'famous'. People flocked for my autograph – I could never understand this ! I mean, anyone could have scribbled down my name – what was the big deal ? Have you ever noticed how 'camera crazy' celebrities become ? If there is press in the area, they make sure to be standing there as well ! Hello !

It still saddens me today to see how status conscious the world has become, and how arrogant the majority of these celebrities are. What happened to looking within and seeing the unique beauty of each and every individual ?

It was a false lifestyle to me and one I did not like, hence I pulled back and focused on the corporate market. Having one to one contact with people again. Inspiring them with the goal of making this world a better place to live in.

Being thankful and aware of even the little pleasures in life is NOT being weak, it is being aware of everything around you and it is about living life in the NOW. Because only if you do this, can you truly enjoy every moment in your day for what it really is.

I would like to end this chapter with two more lessons which I trust will make you look a little more within yourself.

STRUGGLE A LITTLE - THEN FLY !

A man found a cocoon of a butterfly, that he brought home. One day as a small opening appeared, he sat and watched the butterfly for several hours. It struggled to force its body through that little hole. Then it seemed to stop making any progress. It appeared as if it had gotten as far as it could and it could go no farther.

So the man decided to help the butterfly. He took a pair of scissors and snipped off the remaining bit of the cocoon. The butterfly then emerged easily, but, it had a swollen body and small, shriveled wings. He continued to watch the butterfly, he expected that, at any moment, the wings would enlarge and the body would contract. Neither happened !

The butterfly spent the rest of its life crawling around with a swollen body and shriveled wings. It was never able to fly !

The man acted with well-intentioned kindness but he didn't understand the consequences. The restricting cocoon and the struggle required to get through the tiny opening, were nature's way of forcing fluid from the body of the butterfly once it achieved its freedom from the cocoon.

Sometimes struggles are exactly what we need in our life. If we were to go through life without any obstacles, it would cripple us. We would not be as strong as we could have been and we could never fly ?

So the next time you are faced with an obstacle, a challenge, or a problem, remember the butterfly.

Struggle a little - then fly !

DISCOVER YOUR MAGIC

An Obstacle in Our Path by author Unknown

In ancient times, a King had a boulder placed on a roadway. Then he hid himself and watched to see if anyone would remove the huge rock.

Some of the king's wealthiest merchants and courtiers came by and simply walked around it. Many loudly blamed the king for not keeping the roads clear, but none did anything about getting the stone out of the way.

Then a peasant came along carrying a load of vegetables. Upon approaching the boulder, the peasant laid down his burden and tried to move the stone to the side of the road. After much pushing and straining, he finally succeeded.

After the peasant picked up his load of vegetables, he noticed a purse lying in the road where the boulder had been. The purse contained many gold coins and a note from the king indicating that the gold was for the person who removed the boulder from the roadway.

The peasant learned what many of us never understand.

**Every obstacle presents an opportunity
to improve our condition.**

**"The fame of great men ought to be judged always
by the means they used to acquire it."**
Francois de La Rochefoucauld

139

> *"What people say behind your back is your standing in the community."*
>
> **Ed Howe**

> *"A great man is always willing to be little."*
>
> **Ralph Waldo Emerson**

> *"If you live to be a hundred, I want to live to be a hundred minus one day, so I never have to live without you."*
>
> **Winnie the Pooh**

Hence always :

Be open to change
Take action
Smash the routine
Start with small changes

DISCOVER YOUR MAGIC

Notes

A = ASSOCIATIONS

> *"The ladder of success is best climbed*
> *by stepping on the rungs of opportunity."*
>
> **Ayn Rand**

I am going to divide this chapter into two sections, the first dealing with associations as in friendships; business and personal, and the second part dealing with associations as in how to make associations with the world around you to benefit your business.

I have touched on friendships slightly, and mentioned the importance of keeping the mystery going in any relationship. In business it is extremely important to keep all associations on a professional level. Furthermore, it is an advantage when you can get business associates to like you from the word go. This not only makes your job easier, but gives you an advantage over the others.

By now you know a few tips from the chapters on awareness and impressions. An extremely important point I would like to add here is contained in the following story which was told to me a while back. Whether it's true or not, I cannot say, but it's food for thought.

In the New York socialite scene, a wealthy woman invited Dale Carnegie (How to win friends and influence people) to a party. At this time he was well known and a public figure and an absolute 'must have' guest on anyone's party list who was important in the top circles.

On arriving at the hostess's party, she typically went over the top and bombarded him with questions. However, Mr. Carnegie directed all the questions back to her, which resulted in him questioning the hostess about herself. At the end of the night, he had maybe said ten words, and the hostess had spoken most of the evening.

The next day's social section in the newspaper had a comment on Mr. Carnegie's visit and made mention something along line of "He was the hit of the party".

A strange comment, as he didn't say much ! Actually not ! You see, he made the hostess feel important and let her speak about herself the whole evening. At the end of the night, everyone knew everything about her, and not that much more about Mr. Carnegie. Very clever …. Because the nicest thing you can hear besides your name, is your own voice.

And this is exactly what the hostess heard the whole night, making her also feel very special and important. Mr. Carnegie kept some mystery, by never saying much about himself. Hence making him an attractive target on the next invite list.

Do you see my point ?

Don't be self-centred and focus around your life, your product, and your problems. Make a business associate feel important by asking about his/her life. By making them open up to you, they will feel you are interested in them as a person. This will have many further effects, one being that they will automatically like you because you are showing an interest in them.

However, I must warn you, don't try this and not pay full attention. If you intend making them talk and asking about their lives, look interested and show sincerity, otherwise you will only do damage.

DISCOVER YOUR MAGIC

Any experienced salesman will tell you that once you have made your client feel comfortable, and shown an interest in them, it is much easier to sell your product. It's as simple as that.

Often, when the other person starts talking about themselves, he/she answer questions you had planned to pose at a later stage. Thus at the end of the meeting, this person could well think to them self, "What a nice person, he knew exactly what I wanted and didn't even ask me any questions. He was so well prepared and knew just what to say !"

Meanwhile, all you did was listen and nod at the right moment. The rest came naturally ! As a magician I do mind reading tricks, and years ago I played with the concept of cold reading. This means to use psychology, body language and basically all your senses, to extract information from someone. Then simply tell this person what you see. I had to laugh, as people thought I was psychic. But all I was doing was observing and sharing what I saw. The reason I mention this is that this is exactly what a good salesman does – he checks out his client and gives that person what they want.

Your personal relationships also affect your business life. Two weeks after my wife Sonja and I got married, we spent eleven months solid on our first cruise ship as the magic act. For eleven months we shared the same 2 x 2 cabin. Everything that could be picked up and thrown at a person, was thrown at me. Arguments were frequent. It wasn't easy, but we survived. Thereafter that we spent another few years living on other cruise liners, this time, growing closer to each other.

How did we manage this ? Honesty and respect for each other. Yes, you may have heard that 100 times. But how many of you practice honesty with your partners ? If something worries you, don't bottle it up, bring it out in the open right now ! By respecting your partner, you don't belittle or degrade them in any way, but have an adult discussion about any discrepancies or nagging problems that may arise.

 We are all human, and should a heated argument or fight occur, all you need to say is, "I love you". It may be difficult at the time, but whatever you do, be the first to say it ! Even if your partner curses you and goes totally mad. Just keep on saying, "I love you.'

It drove my wife crazy ! To this day, when we speak to others and talk about getting on in a relationship, she is the first to tell people how this would catch her totally off guard. She would be so annoyed with me, and want to throw everything in sight at me, and I pop out with, "I love you."

I know it doesn't solve the issue at hand, but it DOES calm your partner down so that you can now both carry on your argument as a discussion in a normal tone and adult manner. Makes sense, doesn't it ?

People also get complacent with each other. Think back when you met your partner for the first time. One always gave compliments to make the other person feel good, with the aim of this coming back to you in the form of a kiss, cuddle, or you know what !

I find it strange that once the 'hunt' is over, and the 'conquest' has been achieved, compliments are few and far apart. Yes ! We do get used to each other, but if you really sit down and look at your partner and watch them for a while, you will notice many things you can compliment them on. Basically ! Try looking for something new each day to say. Your wife has a cute way she smiles when she puts the kids to sleep, which you never noticed before. Mention it to her. Your husband may not do the dishes every night, but he always tucks in a warm water bottle for you when it's cold – let him know you enjoy this. Even if you think that your partner is the laziest slob around – look for something new, and build on that. This makes your partner feel special and wanted. And they start doing things in return again !

If you have reached the point where you have looked at every part of your partners clothing, behaviour and body. and cannot find anything to compliment them on - compliment them on something ridiculous ! For example, "I have always found your earlobes incredibly attractive." What will happen ? They will laugh and inside they will respect and appreciate the fact that you care enough to always look for something to say to make him/her feel special.

I would like to finish off the first half of this chapter with a quote from an unknown author :

> *"Before criticizing someone, walk a mile in their shoes;*
> *Then when you do criticize them,*
> *you will be a mile away, and have their shoes."*

Today still, I tear out articles from newspapers, airline magazines, trade publications and other periodicals which I think could be useful in my business. I know only a handful of people that do this consciously. with the aim in mind. of furthering their business.

Whatever business you are in, take today's newspaper (preferably a Financial Times, or similar which reports objective business news) and read it carefully and see how many articles, adverts and items you can find that are even remotely connected to your work.
For example, myself as a corporate enter-trainer who inspires and entertains clients, reads a newspaper advert for a

146

management company to put forward tenders to run the new International Conference Centre to be built. I work in this industry ! This is a major factor which will influence future bookings for me. Thus I cut this article out, and get in touch with the company at this early stage. Why ? They will need speakers and trainers throughout the developmental stage – plus they will also be able to recommend me to the management company that eventually runs the centre - who in turn will recommend me to clients wanting to use the venue.

On the next page I may see an article on an intended investment conference, to be held with leading business leaders and celebrity speakers. I immediately contact the organisers to offer my services. If everything has been arranged for this year, I make sure I am in their books for the next year and make a note in my diary accordingly. Two months after the current conference, my diary has an entry with the organiser's name and contact details for me to follow up.

The next page may have an article on the poor tourist facilities in my city, and whose authorities will have to institute an industry standard for the quality of services offered. Lots of names are mentioned in this article. I assume they may hold meetings and conferences, and need a conference chairman, or continuity person who has international travel experience to assist in this matter. I will contact everyone involved and market my services to them. I will tear these out and stick them behind my desk next to my goals list. Sometimes it looks really messy against the wall. This in turn forces me to take action on these articles and follow through, so that I can neaten up the wall again !

Consider a mass mail shot for one moment. What's your response rate on this ? Maybe 1%. By being aware of related articles associated with your industry, and taking action on them, your response rate can suddenly increase to 60% and over.

I have given you 3 examples of how I read the paper. Don't just see newspapers as bringers of bad news and financial facts. In fact, the newspaper to me is like a contact list. Every day I can make at least one business contact. Instead of wasting money on advertising that brings little returns, here you have a medium which gives you regular leads within your field of work.

At all business class lounges in airports around the world, there are usually tons of free business magazines. When I am sitting waiting for a plane – what better opportunity to use the time productively and look for contacts. I have landed many international presentations this way. In the same vein, if like me, you are a frequent flyer – where do you think you will make all your business contacts ? Economy, or business class ? The answer should be obvious !

I have a career which most people don't even consider to be a job - and this works for me. So why can't you pick up the paper and use it 100 times more productively than myself ?

Make associations with everything around you. Becoming aware will make you see gaps in the market from which you can benefit with your product or service.

Never underestimate the power of this, and the opportunity of furthering your dreams by making associations with everything around you. I have found that there have been times when I have thought that an article doesn't really have anything to do with what I offer, or I just had a feeling that I probably shouldn't even bother with it. In fact I wonder why I even kept it ?

Strangely enough, these are always the ones that have brought in more work than the others !

It's all about WHAT I HAVE LEARNT in life. Numerous people have contributed their life lessons in the next example :

WHAT I HAVE LEARNT !

I've learned....That sometimes all a person needs is a hand to hold and a heart to understand.

I've learned....That simple walks with my father around the block on summer nights when I was a child did wonders for me as an adult.

I've learned....That life is like a roll of toilet paper. The closer it gets to the end, the faster it goes.

I've learned....That money doesn't buy class.

I've learned....That it's those small daily happenings that make life so spectacular.

I've learned...That under everyone's hard shell is someone who wants to be appreciated and loved.

I've learned....That the Creator didn't do it all in one day. What makes me think I can?

I've learned....That to ignore the facts does not change the facts.

I've learned....That when you plan to get even with someone, you are only letting that person continue to hurt you.

I've learned....That love, not time, heals all wounds.

I've learned....That the less time I have to work with, the more things I get done.

I've learned....That life is tough, but I'm tougher.

I've learned....That the easiest way for me to grow as a person is to surround myself with people smarter than I am.

I've learned....That everyone you meet deserves to be greeted with a smile.

I've learned....That no one is perfect until you fall in love with them.

I've learned....That opportunities are never lost; someone will take the ones you miss.

I've learned....That when you harbor bitterness, happiness will dock elsewhere.

I've learned....That I wish I could have told my Dad that I love him one more time before he passed away.

I've learned....That one should keep his words both soft and tender, because tomorrow he may have to eat them

I've learned....That a smile is an inexpensive way to improve your looks.

I've learned....That everyone wants to live on top of the mountain, but all the happiness and growth occurs while you're climbing it.

I've learned....That the best classroom in the world is at the feet of an elderly person.

I've learned....That just one person saying to me, "You've made my day !" makes my day.

I've learned....That when you're in love, it shows.

I've learned....That being kind is more important than being right.

I've learned....That you should never say "no" to a gift from a child.

I've learned....That no matter how serious your life requires you to be, everyone needs a friend to act goofy with.

"The tragedy of life is not so much what men suffer, but rather what they miss."
Thomas Carlyle

"A fact in itself is nothing. It is valuable only for the idea attached to it, or for the proof which it furnishes."
Claude Bernard

"My mother said to me, 'If you become a soldier, you'll be a general; if you become a monk, you'll end up as the pope.' Instead, I became a painter and wound up as Picasso."   **Pablo Picasso**

In conclusion :

Show a sincere interest
Honesty and Respect
Always look for something new
Make associations with everything around you

Notes

DISCOVER YOUR MAGIC

L = LAUGHTER

> *"Veni, Vidi, Velcro' - I came, I saw, I stuck around."*
>
> **RL**

How often do you laugh ? Every day ? Or can't you remember the last time a smile crossed you face ?

Laughter is the best medicine !

Boy ! Do I believe this. I want you to sit and think for a moment, how many people did you see today that laughed ? Ninety nine percent of people are stuck in a rut and simply go through the motions. It drives me crazy. If you have ever sat on the tube such as in London's underground, and watched the faces around you - what have you noticed ?

People don't smile, nor do they make eye contact. So here is what I want you to do. The next time you are in a plane, train, bus or anywhere where there are lots of people standing together, I want you to smile at someone.

Guess what is going to happen ? They **will** smile back. In fact, if the smile comes from within and it is sincere, I guarantee that any stranger will smile back. Laughter is infectious, so imagine entering the London underground laughing. Everyone in that tube carriage will have a smile on their faces within a short space of time, and everyone will walk off the tube feeling better. Why they feel better they won't know, they just feel better !

I'll tell you the reason - laughter is medicine ! There have been numerous studies which have proven that people who laugh more are healthier, live longer and have a general better attitude to life. Other studies where done on people who use antidepressants. It was even found that most of these people wouldn't need them if they laughed more everyday ! I once asked an audience what the biggest selling drug in the US was for depression ... and some 'smart aleck' answered, "Cocaine !" The real answer is, Prozac. Lots of people are making lots of money out of this. I have the Prozac replacement solution !

LAUGHTER !

What is more, laughter is positive, and draws positive energy. Remember the brief points on energy in the chapter on Awareness ? Sour and negative people won't hang around jolly people, they draw their own bitter types toward them. I am sure you know a joker amongst your circle of friends or at work. The people he attracts are those that enjoy a laugh.

I have worked with so many retired people. There are many that are bitter, for whatever reason they choose. However, there are many, who come from exactly the same backgrounds and upbringings, who are what I call, "naughty", like little children. They laugh and are in a sense mischievous. These older folk always attract younger people around them, have more fun and enjoy the last part of their lives to the fullest.

Of course I am not saying that you must laugh your problems and life's serious situations away. But, try and look at the lighter side of serious situations.
Einstein put it nicely :

> *"Sit next to a pretty girl for an hour, it seems like a minute.*
> *Sit on a red-hot stove for a minute, it seems like an hour.*
> *That's relativity."*

As a rule in my life I have to laugh every day ! In fact I start my day with a laugh as I am subscribed to a few email joke lists. The first thing I do when I get into my office, is download my mail and read my jokes. It just starts me off in the right mood.

Go onto the world wide web, using any search engine such as google, or yahoo. Simply type in "Free Jokes". Most sites simply ask you to send them an email with "subscribe" in the heading, or let you subscribe there and then. The majority of these lists are absolutely FREE. They won't cost you one single cent ! And every morning you will receive two to three great jokes in your mailbox !

A friend of mine is into clothes designing and opened a shop a few years ago off Rodeo Drive in Beverly Hills. He was a no-name, compared to the big designers in that area. He had to think of a novel way of attracting people into his store. Firstly he believed his designs were as good, if not better than what the other shops offered, but this alone didn't help pay the rent and draw the customers.

He came up with a brilliant idea. Instead of normal mirrors in the shop, he had these circus type mirrors which make you look fat, small, thin, and generally all sorts of funny shapes. Years ago these were popular at fun fairs and was sold as the "Hall of Mirrors" attraction to make you laugh. Well, everyone who came into the store obviously stood in front of these mirrors, and laughed ! Whether they bought clothes or not, they laughed. When they left the store, they were in a better mood, than when they entered. Hence everyone leaving the shop had good memories associated with their visit, besides the novelty factor of the mirrors. They told their friends, and in the end, everyone came to his store.

All he did was add the element of laughter – and he made a big success !

Ladies, apparently a smile uses around 8 muscles in the face, and laughter uses around 21 facial muscles. So why bother with expensive face creams and facial exercises when all you need to do is laugh the whole time and your face will get all the exercise it needs !

Seriously though, if you laugh only once per day more than you do at present, it will affect your mood, thoughts and health in a positive way. If only people laughed more, the whole world would be a happier place. Do you see successful people moping around ? No ! They smile and are excited about life, their future ideas and plans.

So ! Just imagine if you apply everything you have learnt in this book, plus have a specific goals list. If you believe in the saying, "If you can dream it, you can achieve it" – that thought alone is worth smiling about ?

 I went to the doctor the other day and he said to me, "Wolfgang, I haven't seen you in weeks ?" I replied, "I know, I have been sick !"

So he asked, "What's your problem then ?"
I said, " Doctor, I have this recurring dream ! All I dream about is the 'Green Green Grass of Home' !"
He said, "Oh that's no problem ... you have the Tom Jones syndrome !"
Shocked, I queried, " The what ?"
He repeated, " The Tom Jones Syndrome !"
I asked, "Is it rare ?"
And he replied, " Well, it's not unusual !"

THE VALUE OF A SMILE by Author unknown

A smile cost nothing, but gives much.

It enriches those who receive, without making poorer those who give.

It takes but a moment, but the memory of it sometimes lasts forever.

None is so rich or mighty that he can get along without it, and none is so poor that he can be made rich by it.

A smile creates happiness in the home, fosters goodwill in business, and is the countersign of friendship.

It brings rest to the weary, cheer to the discouraged, sunshine to the sad, and is nature's best antidote for trouble.

Yet it cannot be bought, begged, borrowed, or stolen, for it is something that is of no value to anyone until it is given away.

Some people are too tired to give you a smile. Give them one of yours, as none needs a smile so much as he who has no more to give.

Do yourself a favour, just smile at someone from within and watch their reactions. I guarantee you – you will get a smile in return. Next time you are at the post office, driving through a toll booth or government department, where everything and everyone is dull and grey – just smile at the person opposite you ! I bet you'll get really great service ... and make someone else's job day for them !

DISCOVER YOUR MAGIC

What better way to finish off this chapter with some 'funny' inspirational sayings :

"Two things are infinite: the universe and human stupidity; and I'm not even sure about the universe."
Albert Einstein

The Arabs have a saying,
"Trust in God, but tie your camel !"

"To let a fool kiss you is stupid.
To let a kiss fool you is worse."
Unknown

"If women didn't exist,
all the money in the world would have no meaning."
Aristotle Onassis

"If quitters never win, and winners never quit,
what fool came up with, 'Quit while you're ahead'?"
Unknown

"Some see the cup as half full, others see it as half empty.
I just see it as one more thing I have to wash."
Unknown

I would like to end this book with two inspirations and a quote from **Florence Nightingale**. There are many great quotes, and of those, there are a few which really hit the nail on the head. I believe this one to be one of those few.

> *"I contribute my success to this :*
> *I never gave or took an excuse."*

And now the two inspirations :

If A Dog Was The Teacher
You would learn stuff like :

- *When loved ones come home – always run & greet them.*
- *Never pass up the opportunity to go for a joy ride.*
- *Allow the experience of fresh air & wind in your face to be pure ecstasy.*
- *When it's in your best interest, practice obedience.*
- *Let others know when they have invaded your territory.*
- *Take naps and stretch before rising.*
- *Run, romp and play daily.*
- *Thrive on attention and let people touch you.*
- *Avoid biting when a simple growl will do.*
- *On hot days, drink lots of water & lie under a shady tree.*
- *If you're happy, dance around & wag your entire body.*
- *No matter how often you're scolded, don't buy into the guilt thing and pout – run right back and make friends.*
- *Eat with enthusiasm. Stop when you have had enough.*
- *Be loyal – never pretend to be someone you're not.*
- *When someone is having a bad day, be silent, sit close and nuzzle them gently.*

THINGS I WISH I'D KNOWN BEFORE
I WENT OUT IN THE REAL WORLD

No books will be as good as the ones you loved as a child.

Never give yourself a haircut after 3 martinis, or 3 margaritas, or 3 shots of Tequila, or ......?

When baking, follow directions. When cooking, go by your own taste.

Never continue dating anyone who is rude to the waiter.

Good sex should frequently involve laughter. Why ? Because it's, you know ... funny.

If you tell a lie, don't believe it deceives only the other person.

The five most essential words for a healthy, vital relationship:
"I apologize" and "You are right".

Everyone seems normal until you get to know them.

When you make a mistake, make amends immediately. It's easier to eat pie while it's still warm.

The only really good advice that I remember my mother ever gave me was "Go. You might meet somebody."

If he says that you are too good for him - believe it.

The shortest line is always the longest.

Never pass up an opportunity to pee.

DISCOVER YOUR MAGIC

I've learned to pick my battles; I ask myself : "Will this matter one year from now ? How about one month ? One week ? One day ?"

During hard times I ask myself : "How do I feel ? What do I want ?" I use it whenever I'm at a loss for words or thoughts.

If you woke up breathing, congratulations. You have another chance.

If you move far from your family when you're young, consider choosing a career with an airline. Your need to see your family will last a lifetime, as will your travel benefits.

Living well really is the best revenge.

Being miserable because of a bad or former relationship just proves that the other person was right about you.

Be really nice to your friends because you never know when you are going to need them to empty your bed urinal and hold your hand.

Being happy doesn't mean every thing's perfect; it just means you've decided to see beyond the imperfections.

Some people are working backstage, some are playing in the orchestra, some are onstage singing, some are in the audience as critics, and some are there to applaud.

DISCOVER YOUR MAGIC

DISCOVER YOUR MAGIC

M
MOTIVATION

A
AWARENESS

G
GOALS

I
IMPRESSIONS

C
CHANGE

A
ASSOCIATIONS

L
LAUGHTER

BACK-WORD

All books have forewords, but I have never seen a book with a 'back-word' before. Hence in conclusion I have a 'back-word' for you.

It has been my goal to change people's lives for the better through my speaking and now this book. I have written it simplistically and trust that no matter who you are, you have understood the core of my message.

Even if you only use one of the points I discussed, and this brings about a positive change in your life, I will have achieved my goal.

I also know, that no matter how simplistic I make everything sound, it is difficult for many people to put the information into practice. No one is expecting you to become a positive junkie over night. However, if you're just open to the information and start implementing it in small doses (remember : start with small changes) – this will make it easier for you.

Thank you for spending your precious time with me and reading what I have to say.

May your life be filled with all the dreams you desire, and may you have the strength and courage to make them come true.

> *"May the magic in your soul,*
> *lead to the magic in your life !"*
> **Wolfgang Riebe**

FREE OFFER

Monthly Inspiration

It is my desire to keep you inspired for as long as possible. Should you wish to receive an inspirational email from me once per month, **absolutely free of charge**, it will be my honour to make you part of this venture.

My promise to you – I will never sell your email address to anyone, nor will I ever send you any advertising or pictures.

Once per month I will send you a page containing 2 or 3 touching inspirational stories which you can share with colleagues and friends. I promise to do this absolutely free of charge and for the rest of my life. And remember, … your email address will never be traded or sold !

Ideally, log onto my website, www.theriebeinstitute.com and a pop up will appear on the home page where you can fill in your details.

Alternatively, click on the **"Free Motivation"** button, go to that page and add your details here. PLUS - here you can download my **FREE Inspirational E-Book** as well.

And if all else fails, send me an email to :
info@theriebeinstitute.com with **"Subscribe"** in the heading.

That's it … the ball's in your court now !

WOLFGANG RIEBE
A BRIEF BACKGROUND

Whether you need a Keynote Speaker, Trainer, Master of Ceremonies, or a hilarious, baffling Comedy Cabaret Illusionist, Wolfgang will turn the whole event into an unforgettable, sophisticated experience in either English, German, Flemish or Afrikaans.

117 Countries, from the USA to Russia to Iceland. Every major city in the world from Singapore to Istanbul.

Wolfgang is one of a handful of magicians who has achieved fame & fortune by following his dream. To describe his shows' content as 'magic tricks' would be akin to saying, "Mozart had a few catchy tunes !" 'Magician' is definitely not the word that describes him. Incredible tricks designed around your company needs. Coupled with a business suit and sophisticated, up-market, tasteful and passionate presentations makes him arguably one of the top corporate magicians in the world !

Author of over 20 books, and honorary member of some of the oldest and most prestigious magical societies globally. He has lectured and shared his successes with the London Magic Circle, Hollywood's Academy of Magic Arts and performed regularly at the Magic Castle. His is the only South African magician contracted by The Magical Academy of Arts in Hollywood to have ever done this, and is the most successful magician in the history of South Africa and the African continent. He can be considered a 'professor' in his field with hundreds of articles written for many of the most established magical publications in the USA and England.

Besides appearing in leading theatres, international hotel chains,

166

London's West End, spectacular Vegas & Broadway production shows, he has also played global hot-spots for the British forces. One of a handful of magicians who boasts many of his own TV shows from BBC, ETV to SABC. He has appeared in motion pictures, in TV commercials and worked on the world's top 5 star plus cruise liners as a head-line act, including Princess Cruises (Love Boat), Cunard's QE2 & Vistafjord, Hapag Lloyd's Hanseatic & Bremen, Crystal Cruises Crystal Symphony and many others.

Clever humour and comedy, combined with mind blowing magical effects has resulted in him working for most of the top 500 blue chip companies globally. In fact, his review list looks like the "Who's Who' in the corporate industry. Company products, branding and corporate messages included in his presentations have made him not only an entertainer, but consultant as well.

His global experiences led to the next logical step .... to take his entertainment & academic background and give back to society. Hence he developed numerous inspirational talks based on personal global experiences, coupled with teachable, practical life skills which delegates can implement immediately. These include, surviving running aground near the North Pole, watching Krakatoa erupt, exploring the Ice Cap in Greenland, diving the Cayman Fault, walking with the penguins in the Antarctic, experiencing the Bermuda Triangle and sailing force 12 hurricanes in the Atlantic. Coupled this with his unique entertainment style make for unforgettable & informative teachings. From 1 hour keynote presentations to whole day training seminars.

His shows and talks are often combined with the role of Master of Ceremonies, Continuity Person and Conference Chairman. In today's "seen it all" corporate environment, what a delight to find an Emcee who is much more than a "link-man". Versatile

DISCOVER YOUR MAGIC

enough to adapt and change his dialogue & show around your company's requirements. Fluent in many languages, with the experience to host your Annual Awards Evening, your 3 day conference, and all other corporate events - as Speaker, MC and Illusionist.

Today he is one of the busiest and most successful speakers and entertainers on the international circuit ! As a self made business man, he also has a degree in Psychology and Communications, plus a Business Management Diploma. He is the Director of a Television Production and a Property Development Company, and founder of The Riebe Institute with offices worldwide.

He is not just a TV celebrity. He is part of a select group of entertainers globally who have achieved the status of being the 'star' of not one, but numerous of their 'own' prime time TV series. Amongst which were Abracadabra and Master Magician Wolfgang Riebe.

If you want a success story at your next event, Wolfgang will inspire you with his special brand of fine magic and inspiration.

A man that is truly passionate about what he does.

Would you like Wolfgang to appear at your next function ?

Visit his website : **www.theriebeinstitute.com** for more details on what he has on offer, or contact his offices on email:

info@theriebeinstitute.com

LIFE LESSONS
FOR THE
HEART

For many years Wolfgang has collected and shared inspirational stories, anecdotes and sayings in his Free Inspirational Monthly 'Use Letter'. This book contains a collection of these which will not only touch your heart, but give you food for your soul.

An ideal bedside book, or gift for someone you care about.

Most stories are only one page long, yet have so much depth that just reading one insight per day will give new meaning to life.

If you want to put your life back into perspective, be inspired, and find the magic within yourself again, this book is the answer.

If you are not sure whether this book is for you, why not subscribe for <u>Free</u> to Wolfgang's Monthly Inspirational 'Use Letter' and get a taste of what is in this book.

ISBN : 144041212X

Visit : www.theriebeinstitute.com to place your order

POWER CHARGE
YOUR MEMORY
on DVD

**This will be by far one of the most AWESOME, FUN and
LIFE CHANGING DVD's you will ever own !**

Wolfgang teaches a simple and easy to understand technique which
stimulates the neurotransmitters in your brain, thus increasing your
memory.

This technique can be applied to all levels of business and will have a
positive effect on your daily life.

No more 'To Do' lists will ever be needed !
You will be able to remember countless things in your mind !
No more diaries needed to remember appointments !
You will be able to learn new skills much simpler and faster !
Remembering names & faces of clients & friends will be easy !

Wolfgang guarantees that he will improve their memory by at least
200%. The entire pace of the DVD is relaxed, funny and entertaining.
watch the DVD only once ! and you will already have an improved
memory and **can immediately begin applying their new life skill !**

Visit : www.theriebeinstitute.com to place your order

RE-DISCOVER THE
LOST SPARK
IN YOUR RELATIONSHIP

After speaking to, and helping thousands of couples re-discovering the romance in their relationships, Wolfgang has just launched his latest book. Whether you feel you are lacking that 'spark' in your marriage, or even if you feel that everything is great. This book will teach you how to take your relationship to new heights !

Do you want to bring the romance and spice back into your marriage ?

Then this book is a 'Must Read'

Everything is covered, from learning to be more romantic,
understanding each other as a couple,
honest communication, fun ideas and adult play.

It is an easy to read, 'must have' for any couple !

A deeply insightful guide which will enable you
to Discover the Magic of truly Romantic Relationships.

ISBN : 1438292015

Visit : www.theriebeinstitute.com to place your order

450 HOME BUSINESS IDEAS

The global economy is in constant turmoil. Money is becoming tight. Everyone is searching for ideas to ease the global downturn. and put some extra cash in their pockets.

Well, here's the answer ! A book containing OVER 450 Home Business Ideas which you can start part time. The majority of ideas need no start up capital whatsoever. YES, you read correctly ! From home, part time and none, if minimal start up capital.

Most of the business ideas you should be able to start right away, or in a few days. And most of them you need no prior experience, and if you do, you can learn it in a day or two.

This book has been written for those of you looking for an extra income on the side. Those of you who want to work for yourself and become independent. Those of you who are tired of the rat race. Those of you who are just looking for that extra money every month to make ends meet, pay the bills and still have some spending money !

ISBN : 1440412146

Visit : www.theriebeinstitute.com to place your order

WORKING ON CRUISE SHIPS AS AN ENTERTAINER

So you want work on a cruise ship as an entertainer ! What's it like ? What types of contracts are available ? What is expected of you ? Ship life – what's it all about ? How much do they pay ? How many shows do you need ? What kind of accommodation do they offer ?

Everything you ever wanted to know about working on a cruise liners is covered. Plus contact addresses of cruise companies and agents ! Being informed of all the ins and outs of this industry will enable you to make the right choices and decisions before starting on your first ship.

Wolfgang Riebe worked as a headline act on many of the world's top 5 star plus cruise liners. From Cunard's QE2 and Vistafjord to Hapag Lloyd's Hanseatic & Bremen. From the original Princess Cruises 'Love Boat' to the Royal and Sky Princess. The Song of Flower, Crystal Symphony, Star Odyssey, Marco Polo and Gripsholm were all home to Wolfgang & his wife for many years. From cabaret Comedy Illusion shows to full spectacular Broadway and Vegas style extravaganzas. Wolfgang truly lived the life of a successful cruise ship head line act, literally circumnavigating the globe many, many times over.

ISBN : 144042912X

Visit : www.theriebeinstitute.com to place your order

ONE LINERS YOU WILL USE

Alphabetically categorized !

Over 2000 quick funny one liner jokes !

Ideal for professional Speakers, entertainers and comedians.

One liners you will use is an A to Z of snappy, funny one liner gags that you will be able to inject into your own show. Between the covers of Wolfgang's book is a whole battery of one liners, all suitable for the right occasion. These one liners are all carefully categorized according to subject and so it is an easy, quick reference method of finding the right gag for the right spot in your magic show.

Take advantage of years of practical experience going into this book. Imagine how long it would take of real live performance to find all these gags that work – and that is the beauty of the book – they ARE gags that work.

ISBN : 1438221053

Visit : www.theriebeinstitute.com to place your order

Notes